Crikey!

A RANDOM HOUSE BOOK published by
Random House New Zealand
18 Poland Road, Glenfield, Auckland, New Zealand

For more information about our titles go to
www.randomhouse.co.nz

A catalogue record for this book is available from the National
Library of New Zealand

Random House New Zealand is part of the Random House Group
New York   London   Sydney   Auckland   Delhi   Johannesburg

First published 2009
© text, Richard Wolfe, 2009; images, copyright remains with the
individual copyright holders as listed on page 288

Permission to use the Mr. Four Square image granted by Foodstuffs
(Auckland) Ltd. and Icon Images NZ Ltd., www.mrfoursquare.co.nz

Every effort has been made to contact the copyright holders of
the images in this book. If you have any information about the
copyright of the images in this book please contact the publishers.

The moral rights of the author have been asserted
ISBN 978 1 86979 066 0

This book is copyright. Except for the purposes of fair reviewing
no part of this publication may be reproduced or transmitted in
any form or by any means, electronic or mechanical, including
photocopying, recording or any information storage and retrieval
system, without permission in writing from the publisher.

Design: Nick Turzynski
Four Square man illustration by Nick and Conrad Turzynski
Printed in China by Everbest Printing Co Ltd

Talk about Kiwiana

Richard Wolfe

RANDOM HOUSE
NEW ZEALAND

'Crikey' – and 'crikey dick' – are exclamations of surprise or astonishment. 'Crikey' is derived from the word 'Christ', and as a similar sounding substitute it avoids the use of a profanity. The more emphatic 'crikey dick' has nothing to do with King Dick (Richard John Seddon), but is a euphemism for the Devil.

'Crikey' was in use in Britain in the 1830s and brought to New Zealand by the 1860s. An early appearance in print here was in a poem published in the *Nelson Examiner and New Zealand Chronicle* newspaper in 1863, while a report on the exhibits at the 1875 Agricultural and Horticultural Show at Hokitika claimed the cabbages were so 'fearful and wonderful' they would provoke exclamations of 'crikey'.

contents

- Quarter-acre paradise 6
- Corker grub 25
- A fine drop 51
- Glad rags 60
- At the chalkface 73
- Crouch, touch engage 87
- Fair dinkum fun 106
- Up the boohai 134
- Tangata whenua 144
- 159 Godzone country
- 172 Gummint
- 190 Number-eight wire
- 204 Cow cockies
- 229 Hard yakker
- 247 Pedal to the metal
- 260 Go bush
- 273 The shaky isles
- 288 Image credits

Quarter-ACRE paradise

Do-it-yourself

New Zealand is a nation of handymen and handywomen. This involves doing jobs around the home — such as building garden sheds and repairing cars — rather than paying someone else to do it. A 1983 guide book for people planning to immigrate advised that 'do-it-yourself is a New Zealand pastime'.

The popularity of DIY in New Zealand resulted in new laws in 2008 which meant that people building their own homes would be responsible for the quality of their workmanship for a period of 10 years.

Kiwi can-do and Kiwi ingenuity

New Zealanders like to think they are blessed with a native creativity known as Kiwi ingenuity. This is based on the belief that the early arrivals in this country — Maori and European — needed to be able to make things from limited resources.

Benzine and kerosene tins

Benzine was the common (American) name for petrol in this country until the 1940s. It was available here long before New Zealanders were driving cars and by 1864 was being sold by glass and paint suppliers.

Kerosene, usually known as kero, was used for lighting and heating in New Zealand from the early 1860s.

Kerosene and benzine were sold in four-gallon tins that came in pairs packed in a wooden case. Once emptied, these tins and cases were often put to further use. Useful items that could be made from old benzine tins included feeding trays for lambs and troughs for other animals, as well as cheap and practical furniture for around the home.

Quarter-acre section

The common size of a New Zealand suburban section is the quarter acre, which is around 1000 square metres. This size was popular in the early days because it was considered large enough to provide for the then-essential household vegetable garden. The idea of New Zealanders conforming to a standard-sized section was reflected in the title of a 1972 book, Austin Mitchell's *The Half-gallon Quarter-acre Pavlova Paradise*.

44-gallon drum

Oil and petrol came in 44-gallon drums and 40-gallon drums that, with a bit of Kiwi can-do, were refashioned into useful objects for use around the farm and home. The battered drums were used by Ministry of Works gangs to warn motorists of road works ahead, and for incinerators and rubbish bins. A 1930s book described how to make a large number of useful items from empty 44-gallon drums, including a wheelbarrow and a water cart.

Sugarbags

During the Depression of the late 1920s and 1930s, empty sugarbags made of fine sacking were reworked into many different household

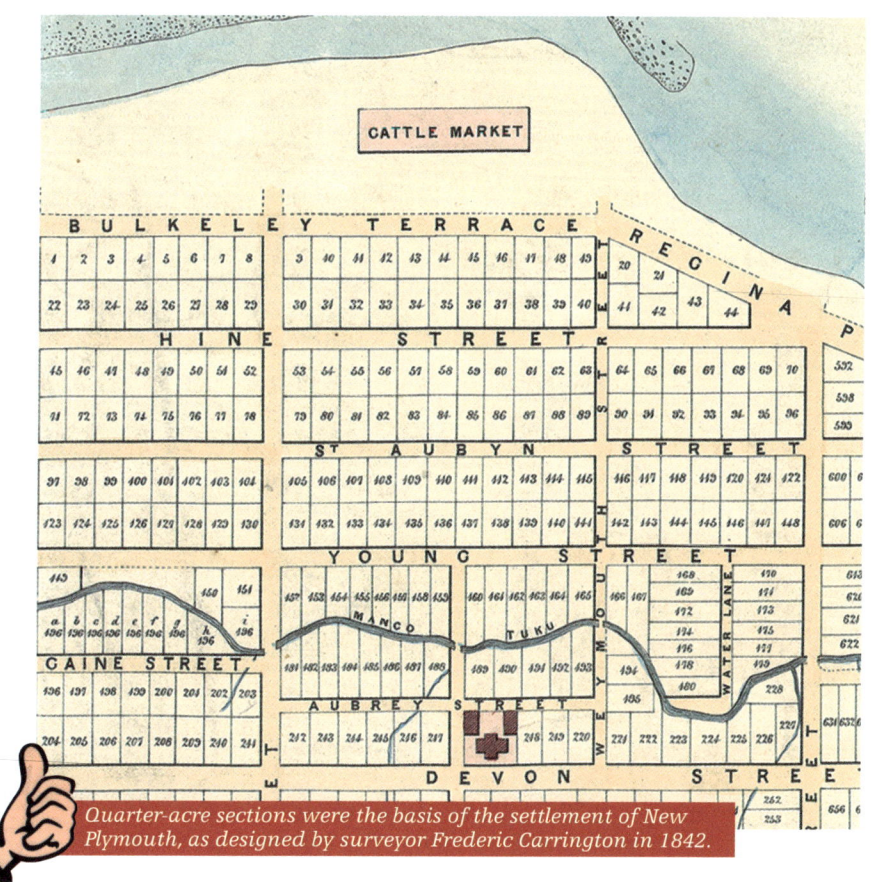

Quarter-acre sections were the basis of the settlement of New Plymouth, as designed by surveyor Frederic Carrington in 1842.

Quarter-acre PARADISE

items, such as carry bags, aprons and oven cloths. In 1974 Tony Simpson entitled his book on this period of our history *The Sugarbag Years*, and the term came to symbolise the poverty and the necessary 'making do' of the time.

Butterflies

In the 1950s many houses around New Zealand were decorated with large wooden butterflies. These colourful insects were attached to the outside front wall of otherwise unadorned houses, and were clearly visible from the street.

Verandah

The verandah, an open-sided roofed structure attached to a house, probably originated in India. The idea was taken to Australia in the early 1800s and it later became a common feature of New Zealand houses, as well.

Back yard

The part of a New Zealand section behind the house which usually includes a vegetable garden, chook-house, clothes-line and back shed that are, generally, not visible from the street — unlike the usually much tidier front part of the section.

Butter boxes

Butter was packed for transport in wooden boxes made of kahikatea, which did not taint the butter. These boxes also had uses around the

It is likely this fashion for house decoration came to New Zealand via Australia. In fact, real butterflies have also been blown across the Tasman on strong westerly wind currents.

home and were turned into bookcases and other items of furniture, especially during the Depression.

Lawnmowing

Traditionally, the typical New Zealand house was set back far enough from the street to allow for a front lawn, which needed mowing, and a flower garden. In 1910 two Aucklanders, Reuben Porter and Harold Mason, went into business manufacturing vacuum pumps and engines for farm equipment. Mason and Porter Ltd., or Masport, became a household name in 1930 when it launched its first lawnmower, to be pushed by hand. The company produced its first cylindrical, power-driven handmower in 1938.

Barbecue

The barbecue or barbie is a popular feature of the New Zealand back yard. Weather permitting, it allows for casual outdoor cooking and eating. The practice was probably introduced from Australia, where the barbecue has been described as a national icon. The barbie is largely a male domain and usually involves sausages, steak and chops, although a beach barbie will often include the catch of the day.

Chooks

Chooks — from the word 'chickens' — is the popular name for domesticated poultry, including hens, chickens and fowls. They were first brought to New Zealand by the Reverend Samuel Marsden in 1814. By 1960, when there were about four million such birds here, most suburban back yards had a chook-house — also known as a chook-run, fowl house or fowl yard. Families enjoyed a year-round supply of fresh eggs and feeding the chooks was usually the responsibility of younger members of the family.

Nowadays, fewer New Zealanders have the room, or inclination, to have a back-yard chook-run. But for those that do, there are now a few rules. For example, residents of Auckland City are allowed to keep six chickens, but no roosters. There are also some strict requirements concerning the construction, maintenance and location of a chook-house and run.

Sleepouts and granny flats

Sleepouts began appearing on New Zealand sections in the 1970s as small out-buildings separate from the main house. Some are relocatable cabins, and most are used for additional sleeping accommodation or as offices or studios.

A granny flat is a self-contained minor dwelling on the same section as another larger major dwelling or house. Mostly they are used by an elderly family member, although many are now occupied by teenagers or 20-something offspring who want a degree of independence, while being handy to other family members.

Home milk deliveries

Until the late 1980s, New Zealanders living in towns and cities enjoyed home milk deliveries. Empty glass bottles were placed at the gate, along with the correct number of milk tokens — made of plastic or pressed metal — for the milkman to swap for full bottles. Bottles ranged in size from the large quart, down to the pint and half-pint, while there was an even smaller one for cream. Eventually, as the bottles gave way to plastic and cardboard containers, home deliveries also began to disappear and New Zealanders began buying their milk solely from the dairy or supermarket.

Rural mail delivery

Until 1905, when the rural delivery service was introduced, New Zealanders living beyond the range of the postman had to collect their own mail from their local post office. Later, mail was delivered to outlying country areas and by 1922 there were 8700 private letterboxes using the rural mail delivery service. The letters 'RD' indicated a rural delivery address, and were often followed by a number which indicated the route number, as in RD2. Rural road-side letterboxes are made from all sorts of things, including old milk or cream cans, and many have become interesting features of their community.

Soap

In 1884 William Hesketh Lever of Lancashire produced the world's first-ever soap that was imprinted with its brand name — Sunlight. It proved so popular that within four years he built the world's largest soapworks to keep up with the demand. By the end of the 1880s his company, now Lever Brothers, was making Sunlight in Sydney. Soon afterwards the organisation opened a factory in Petone, just north of Wellington, and began making Sunlight here.

Levers of Petone also produced other products that became household names, including Rinso, Lux, Lifebuoy and Knight's Castile. Today the Petone factory employs 250 staff and produces some 50,000 tonnes of laundry powder, including Persil, Surf, Drive and Omo, for the Australasian market.

Taniwha soap

Taniwha laundry soap first appeared in the late nineteenth century and it is still the best known commercial application of the mythical Maori water monster. In 1905 a box of 16 bars cost 16/6 (16 shillings and sixpence) and the soap was described as 'the big golden bar of purity'. It was made in Auckland by the Union Oil, Soap and Candle Company,

 *Invented in England in 1884, Sunlight Soap was being manufactured in Petone, north of Wellington, by the end of the century. Over a century later it is still going strong.*

which later moved from Albert Street to be near the freezing works at Westfield, the source of the tallow used to make the soap. Taniwha soap eventually became a victim of automatic washing machines and disappeared.

Clever Mary

Available in the first half of the twentieth century, the household cleanser Clever Mary cost 1/- (1 shilling) per tin in 1915. It was advertised as the 'Enemy of Grease' and was said to be good for getting grime off enamel baths, dishes, pots and pans, and woodwork around the kitchen sink. A 1923 advertisement suggested Clever Mary did all the work: 'Let her lighten the task for you . . . See how quickly she removes finger-marks from doors, smudges from paintwork, stains from tables and benches.'

Janola

The liquid bleach was invented by two Aucklanders who named it after their wives — Jan and Nola. Perhaps they were inspired by Harpic, the English bleach which appeared in the 1920s and was named after its inventor, Harry Pickup. Janola was produced by Reckitt & Coleman.

Rinso

Rinso soap powder for clothes was invented in England and made by Lever Brothers of Port Sunlight from 1908. It was one of the first mass-marketed soap powders and was manufactured in New Zealand by Lever Brothers of Petone from 1924. It was heavily advertised nationwide in the 1950s and 1960s on Selwyn Toogood's radio quiz programmes before it, too, fell victim to the automatic washing machine. It disappeared from the New Zealand market in 1982.

Karitane nursing

Karitane is a small town on the east coast of the South Island, about 34 kilometres northeast of Dunedin. In 1889 it was the home of Sir Frederick Truby King who was superintendent of the local mental hospital. In 1907 he founded the Royal New Zealand Society for the Health of Women and Children. The name Karitane was given to

 Crikey!

hospitals established to help mothers and their babies, and nurses trained in looking after babies became known as Karitane nurses.

Beehive matches

In 1933 the English company of Bryant & May, Bell & Co. began manufacturing Beehive brand safety matches at its new factory in Wellington, New Zealand. They quickly proved popular, particularly with the nation's large number of smokers. In 1963 Beehive almost had the New Zealand market to itself when the older type of wax matches were outlawed for fire safety reasons. But soon, changing habits caused a decline in the use of matches, and the Beehive brand was sold to a Swedish company. The matches are now made overseas.

The industrious bee was a popular image for commercial trademarks and products from the nineteenth century. More recently the idea was adopted for New Zealand's favourite children's toy, the Buzzy Bee.

Plunket

Sir Frederick Truby King founded the Royal New Zealand Society for the Health of Women and Children — later renamed Plunket (in honour of Lady Plunket and her husband, the Governor of New Zealand) in 1907 — with a vision to help mothers and save babies suffering from malnutrition and disease. His belief in a scientific approach to nutrition and childcare led to the founding of Plunket clinics and Karitane hospitals to provide for new and expectant mothers and their babies. Plunket celebrated its centennial in 2007 and is New Zealand's largest provider of support services for the development, health and well-being of children under the age of five. Plunket's helpline, which is funded by community and corporate donors, receives about 70,000 inquiries per year.

Cookery books

An estimated 3000 cookery books have been published in New Zealand since the 1890s compared to some 13,000 in Australia. The best known and most enduring has been the *Edmonds Cookery Book*, which first appeared in 1907. Large sections of the early books were given over to recipes for home baking, reflecting the need to be ready for guests who might drop in unannounced.

A large number of books were also produced to raise funds during wartime, such as *Our Boys' Cookery Book,* in aid of the Wounded Soldiers Fund and published in 1915. Also bound to be useful was the *Ultimate Cookery Book* compiled by Aunt Daisy in 1959, with more than 1300 recipes.

Cookery books reflect social changes, too. For example, in the 1960s a combination of the increasing number of New Zealand women entering the workforce and the availability of commercially manufactured biscuits led to a decline in recipes for home baking.

Agee jars

Agee jars are essential for preserving surplus food by bottling. The name — AG — probably refers to the Melbourne company Australian Glass Manufacturers Co. Ltd., which established a factory in Penrose, Auckland, in 1922. This enterprise, which became New Zealand Glass Manufacturers, went on to produce most of the glass containers used in this country. The Agee preserving jar dates from at least the 1940s and is still available in two sizes — small or half litre, and large or one litre.

Bloke

A bloke — also Kiwi bloke and ordinary bloke — used to be another word for a stereotypical New Zealand male, distinguished by his speech, dress and attitudes. Practical and decent, although prejudiced and unimaginative, he was the sort of individual described in novels by Barry Crump. Today, bloke has a more generic meaning — it is simply an alternative word for man, e.g. 'He's a good bloke'.

Joker

From the early days of European settlement New Zealand was familiar with jokers — individuals who were merry and/or played tricks. By the early 1900s the term could mean an ordinary man or bloke. The earlier meaning was apparent in the Supreme Court in Wellington in 1843 when a witness was described as 'a great joker', but one who wouldn't joke about certain subjects.

Arthur Yates

For over a century Yates has been the biggest name in New Zealand gardening. The story began in 1879 when Arthur Yates, from Manchester, England, came to New Zealand for health reasons. He began a seed business in Auckland in 1883, and in the 1890s launched his packets of 'Yates Reliable Seeds' for home gardeners. The product range was soon extended to fertilisers, sprays, pots and tools. In response to gardeners' queries, Arthur wrote and published the first *Yates Garden Guide* in 1895. Regularly updated, it is in its seventy-seventh edition and it qualifies as an all-time best-seller in both New Zealand and Australia.

Crook

In addition to meaning dishonest and bad, in New Zealand 'crook' can also refer to an illness or state of bad health, as in 'feeling crook', and having 'a crook back'. Also, if someone's really angry they might be described as 'going crook'.

Dunny

Dunny is another name for lavatory. Before the development of flush toilets, a dunny — also as known as a long drop — was a small outdoor shelter built with a seat over a hole in the ground. Dike and dyke are other less common names for a dunny.

A young gardener with a packet of Yates 'Reliable Seeds', in 1948. By then Yates had been supplying the vegetable and flower gardens of New Zealand for over 50 years.

Hottie

A hotwater bottle for keeping warm in bed is usually referred to as a hottie for short. These days a hottie is made from rubber and encased in a cloth or woollen covering. It is filled with hot water and tends to remain hot through much of the night. In the nineteenth and early twentieth centuries, hotties were made of metal or earthenware.

Nappy Valley

Nappy Valley is a term which has been given to certain New Zealand suburban areas where there is a large proportion of young couples with children. It was first applied to Wainuiomata, which was developed in the 1950s as part of Lower Hutt, a suburb of Wellington.

Aunt Daisy

Maud Ruby Taylor was born in London in 1879 and as a child she was known as Daisy. She came to New Zealand with her family in 1891, settling in New Plymouth. She trained as a teacher and married civil engineer Frederick Basham. In 1930 she presented a children's holiday programme at the Auckland radio station 1YA. Now known as 'Aunt Daisy', she moved to Wellington in 1937, and began the morning radio session that made her famous. Beginning with a cheery 'Good morning, everybody', she would talk rapidly for an hour on a wide range of subjects. She offered handy hints for housewives, recipes and positive thoughts for the day, and became a household name. She also advertised products, but only those she had tried herself and could (very enthusiastically) recommend. Aunt Daisy also produced numerous books featuring her recipes

and handy hints. A small, dynamic woman, she was made an MBE in 1956. She died in 1963.

Rawleigh's man

In 1932 door-to-door salesmen introduced New Zealanders to products from the Rawleigh's company, which began in America in 1889. The Rawleigh's man carried his stock, including medicinal, nutritional and homecare products (the best known being the tin of antiseptic salve) from door to door. The company still operates, but the 'Rawleigh's man' is likely to have been replaced by a woman or, perhaps, a couple. The Rawleigh organisation now has 350 distributors throughout New Zealand. In a reflection of changing social patterns, more business is now done at local markets than visiting door to door.

Rawleigh's Medicated Ointment, sold door to door and recommended for a wide range of minor complaints.

Solo mum

With the introduction of the DPB (Domestic Purposes Benefit) in 1974, single parents were able to stay home to care for their children and did not have to rely on paid employment. Men were eligible for the DPB, but most of those who claimed it were women. This led to the creation of a new type of New Zealander known as the 'solo mum'.

In November 2008 Paula Bennett, Member of Parliament for Waitakere, was appointed Minister of Social Development. Bennett had earlier been a solo parent, and she was reported to have said she had gone full circle, 'from being a solo mum on the [DPB] to now controlling the benefit purse strings'.

Southern Man

One of New Zealand's most distinctive regional types, epitomised by the Southern Man from Otago and Southland, is a strong, silent Kiwi bloke. He has an understated sense of humour and a preference for the great outdoors over city life. He is celebrated at Dunedin International Airport in the form of a life-sized bronze statue of a working man on a horse, commissioned by Speight's Brewery.

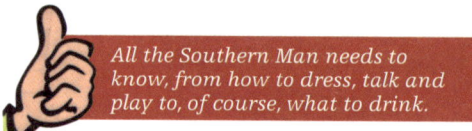

All the Southern Man needs to know, from how to dress, talk and play to, of course, what to drink.

Corker GRUB

Hangi

A hangi is a Maori earth oven and preparing a hangi is usually a communal activity. It is also the name given to the food cooked in a hangi. The raw food is wrapped and placed over hot stones in a hole in the ground. It is covered with mats and earth to keep the heat in to cook the food.

In 1842 a European explorer in the southern part of the North Island described the process: '[a hangi is] an excellent method of cooking; a hole is dug in the earth and a large fire made in it, on which large stones are placed to heat; as soon as the fire has burnt down, the remaining embers are taken out, and some of the hot stones laid carefully round the bottom of the hole, a small quantity of water is then poured on the stones, and the meat laid on them, the remaining hot stones are then laid on the top of the meat, and then a layer of grass; the whole is then covered with earth, so that none of the steam can escape, the meat remains in the hangi for two hours, when the covering is removed, the meat is found dressed in excellent style.'

— *New Zealand Gazette and Wellington Spectator*, 29 June 1842

Kete

Maori used flax or similar leaves to weave baskets known as kete. Kete had a plaited handle on each side, and were used for carrying food. In 1847 an explorer in the central North Island described eating an evening meal of potatoes and fish at a Maori village that was presented: 'according to Native custom, in a small kete or basket

Rising steam, and expectations, as a hangi is opened at Mount Cook School, Wellington, in 1974.

Corker GRUB

made extempore of fresh flax, and which after being used as a plate, is thrown away.'

— *New Zealander*, 3 November 1847

Kumara

The kumara is a sweet potato and was a major food crop for Maori before the arrival of Europeans in New Zealand. When the *Endeavour* was at Cook's Cove, Coromandel, in October 1769, Sydney Parkinson observed 'plantations of Koomarra and Taro' which were 'cultivated with great care, and kept clean and neat'.

The origin of the kumara is a subject of much debate among scientists. One popular theory is that it originated in Central America and was then taken to the various islands around the Pacific. Most of this country's kumara are grown in Northland, and as a result Dargaville describes itself as 'The Kumara Capital of New Zealand'.

Puha

Puha is the Maori name for sow-thistle, a vegetable the Maori cook by boiling. It is often eaten with pork, in the popular dish 'pork and puha'.

Muttonbird

The muttonbird, or sooty shearwater, breeds in the islands to the south of New Zealand. It is known as titi to Maori, who have a legal right to collect the birds for meat from islands off Stewart

Island. The name muttonbird was first used in Norfolk Island where an officer in the Royal Marines once referred to the birds as 'flying sheep'.

Fishing

Fish and shellfish have always provided a rich source of protein to people living in New Zealand. The coastal waters in the early days were abundant with a wide variety of sea life. In 1843 an English woman, who had recently settled in Auckland with her husband, recorded: 'The kinds of fish most commonly brought about here, are the snapper, the mullet, and a fish like our sole in look and taste, but rather smaller. Oysters are sixpence a kit. A kit is a native basket, made of the plaited flax of the country; one may contain from four hundred to five hundred oysters. Cockles, called here pipies, fetch about the same price.'

— *Nelson Examiner and New Zealand Chronicle*, 3 June 1843

Bluff oysters

Bluff, 27 kilometres south of Invercargill, lies at the southern end of State Highway 1 — the name comes from a headland known as The Bluff, on the western side of the entrance to Bluff Harbour. From here, oyster fishermen harvest Bluff oysters in Foveaux Strait. The official season begins on 1 March and finishes on 31 August, with the world-famous annual Bluff Oyster and Food Festival the definite highlight of the season. Bluff oysters are widely regarded as the best in the world.

Pipi

The pipi is an edible shellfish, with a white shell. A popular source of food for Maori, it is found throughout New Zealand, on beaches and in estuaries.

Paua

Known elsewhere in the world as abalone, paua is a shellfish with a vividly coloured iridescent blue and green shell. The flesh is valued as a food by the Maori, whose craftsmen traditionally used the shell for fishing lures and to decorate wooden carvings. The paua shell remains a popular material for the manufacture of souvenirs and jewellery. The whole shells are also sometimes used as ash-trays.

Toheroa

The toheroa is a burrowing clam found on sandy beaches in Southland, on the west coast near Wellington and Dargaville and on Ninety Mile Beach in the Far North. It is considered one of New Zealand's finest seafoods and a canned toheroa soup was once commonly available. Now extremely rare, the toheroa is a protected species and can only be gathered when the Ministry of Fisheries declares a one-day open season at Oreti Beach in Southland.

Whitebait

The small fish known as whitebait is a New Zealand delicacy, and is popularly eaten cooked in fritters. In Europe and other parts of

the world the term whitebait is used for the young of fish, but in New Zealand it refers specifically to the young of the freshwater fish known to the Maori as inanga. Whitebait hatch in the sea and are caught in nets in the lower reaches of rivers when they swim upstream to fresh water.

Whitebaiting is a seasonal activity, but there are strict controls over the size and location of nets, and the fishing season (August November in most parts of the country) is strictly controlled to prevent over-fishing.

Snapper

The snapper is one of the most plentiful and popular eating-fish caught in New Zealand waters. It is found mostly around the North Island, and there is a popular snapper-fishing competition at Ninety Mile Beach each year.

Orange roughy

In the early 1980s New Zealanders first heard about a newly discovered deep-water species of fish. It was called orange roughy because of its rough orange-coloured skin. With its small bones and tasty white flesh, the fish is a valuable export for New Zealand and most are caught near the Chatham Islands.

Butter

Butter has proved of great importance to New Zealanders, both for exporting and home consumption. The first pair of cows was brought to the Bay of Islands in 1824 by the missionary Samuel Marsden. Sixty years later there were nearly 57,000 cows supplying the country's 62 butter factories, of which 26 were located in Taranaki. These factories produced their own brands of butter, the most famous being the Anchor brand.

Exporting butter was made possible with the introduction of refrigerated shipping in 1882. Later, the arrival of home refrigerators made butter easier to store but that made it more difficult to spread. As a result, in the 1970s the New Zealand Dairy Research Institute found a method of producing a non-lumpy spreadable butter. Fifteen years later it became available in the shops, and in 1991 it was successfully launched in the United Kingdom.

Chelsea sugar

In 1882 the New Zealand Sugar Company was formed by a partnership between the Colonial Sugar Refining Company of Australia and others, including New Zealand businessmen. The site chosen for the new business was on the northern shoreline of Auckland's Waitemata Harbour. It was named Chelsea, after the fashionable residential area of London on the north bank of the River Thames. Following construction of the refinery, production of Chelsea sugar began in 1884.

Sure to Rise baking powder

One of New Zealand's most durable and best-known trademarks was established in 1879 when Thomas Edmonds invented his Sure to Rise baking powder. The rising-sun symbol was especially appropriate as

it suggested any baking that included this product was bound to rise — just as the sun does every morning. The rising sun is an ancient symbol, and its radiating rays made it a positive and popular image for products throughout the world in the nineteenth century.

Introduced in 1879, Thomas J. Edmond's distinctive product has been a vital ingredient in New Zealand baking for 130 years.

Highlander milk

The Underwood Milk Preserving Works at Wallacetown, near Invercargill, began making Highlander condensed milk in 1892. The sweet, creamy product was instantly popular in domestic kitchens and commonly used in baking and salad dressings. The Highlander on the label is believed to have been based on the drum major in a Southland pipe band.

Ice cream

New Zealanders are among the biggest ice-cream eaters in the world, not far behind the United States and Australia. In 1996 writer Gilbert Wong calculated that New Zealanders ate enough ice cream each year to fill Auckland's Tepid Baths 146 times over. By 2006 the average New Zealander was eating a little over 22 litres of ice cream and related products each year.

Weet-Bix

One of New Zealand's favourite breakfast cereals originated in the late 1800s when, after much difficulty, a United States manufacturer perfected a healthy wheat-flake biscuit named Granose. It was sold by Sanitarium in New Zealand from the early 1900s. Weet-Bix was introduced in the 1920s by another company, Grain Products. In 1930 Sanitarium bought Grain Products and Weet-Bix went on to become its top product, manufactured in Auckland, Palmerston North and Christchurch.

Sir Edmund Hillary chooses WEET-BIX

Sir Edmund Hillary took Weet-Bix with him on his famous Himalayan expedition. For the same reason, too — because Weet-Bix is so delicious, so full of nourishing goodness, so quick and easy to serve it's with the New Zealand Antarctic expedition. Have your Weet-Bix with hot milk. It's the perfect winter breakfast.

And here's another Weet-Bix scoop —

the story of flight on 50 full-colour picture cards

Fifty free full-colour cards tell the exciting story of the "Evolution of Flight". There are two cards in every large 24-ounce packet of Weet-Bix; one in the 12-ounce size. Start collecting them today.

Sir Edmund Hillary (see page 170), conqueror of Everest, honoured on a Weet-Bix card.

Corker GRUB 35

In 1941 Weet-Bix introduced its first collectors' cards and in 1953 the product received great publicity when it was eaten by Sir Edmund Hillary during his successful expedition to Mount Everest. By the late 1980s Weet-Bix was New Zealand's most popular cereal. The unofficial world Weet-Bix eating record is held by Garry Carpenter of Matamata, who in 1988 managed to munch through 38 biscuits in just 40 minutes.

Creamoata

In 1883 Thomas Fleming bought into a Gore flour mill that had opened in 1878. The new company became Fleming and Co. in 1902 and began producing Creamota — Cream o' the oat — porridge. In 1913 it was advertised as a 'perfect breakfast food'. It was also economical — 'twelve breakfasts for a penny'. From around 1915 this national favourite was promoted by a young, patriotic scout named Sergeant Dan. As 'the Creamota man' he advertised the product until the 1980s, and a large image of Dan long graced the wall of the Gore mill. But in 2001 the owners of Creamota and Sergeant Dan decided to close the local business and transfer oat-milling operations to Australia.

Vogel's bread

In the 1940s a German refugee named Dr Ernst Reizenstein established a bakery on Ponsonby Road, Auckland, making rye and wholegrain breads. One of his employees, Johan Klisser, a war orphan from Holland, bought the business in 1962. He expanded it and obtained the rights to bake Dr Vogel's Swiss-style wholegrain bread, which had been introduced earlier to Australia — Dr Alfred Vogel was a Swiss nutritionist.

After Vogel's bread was no longer made in Australia, it continued to be produced by Klisser's Farmhouse Bakery in south Auckland and it is still a New Zealand favourite. In the 1990s the Vogel's brand was the subject of a series of television advertisements showing young New Zealanders abroad homesick for their favourite bread, or trying to smuggle loaves through Customs. Perhaps as a result, Vogel's bread is now available at certain supermarkets in the United Kingdom.

Marmite

The popular yeast extract Marmite — along with its younger competitor, Vegemite — had its origins in nineteenth century Europe when meat was in short supply. In 1902 the Marmite Food Extract Company was formed at Burton-on-Trent, England, and took its name from *marmite* — the French word for stewpot. English-made Marmite was available in New Zealand by 1903, and in the 1930s it was manufactured locally by the Sanitarium Health Food Company in Christchurch.

Vegemite

Vegemite is a popular breakfast spread in New Zealand. In 1923 Fred Walker of Melbourne, whose company supplied a local brewery with yeast, got his chemist to devise a thick, dark paste combining yeast with several other things, including celery and onions. Vegemite soon became a national favourite. It was first made in this country in 1958, but all our supplies are now made in Melbourne. In October 2008 the Kraft factory passed a milestone when the one-billionth jar of Vegemite came off its production line.

Chesdale cheese

In the days when few New Zealand homes had refrigerators, keeping non-processed cheese fresh was a problem. Chesdale cheese were a processed cheddar and its foil-wrapped triangular segments was popular for school lunches from the 1950s on. In the early 1960s the cheese was promoted by two rural characters, Ches and Dale, dressed in gumboots and black singlets. Around 1968 they appeared in an animated television advertisement, singing a jingle that all New Zealanders soon took up: 'We are the boys from down on the farm, we really know our cheese . . .'

Cheerios and saveloys

A cheerio is a small red-skinned sausage. Cheerios are commonly served at children's parties, and toothpicks are used for dipping them in tomato sauce. The saveloy — more usually known as a 'sav' — is a highly seasoned red-skinned sausage. It was once very popular in New Zealand, often served at after-match sports functions and also eaten with tomato sauce. However, the popularity of the saveloy is on the decline in New Zealand — in 2008 it was no longer one of the household items used to measure the nation's food-price index.

Luncheon sausage

Luncheon sausage is a general name for cured and processed meat shaped into the form of sausage, which is handy for slicing and using as a cheap sandwich filling. It was previously known as German or Belgian sausage, and the term 'luncheon' was introduced as a patriotic replacement during the First World War.

Ches and Dale, the boys from down on the farm who really know their cheese.

Corker GRUB 39

Pies

New Zealand inherited its taste for pies from Britain. In other countries a pie is usually a large dessert to be divided among a number of people, but in New Zealand pies are generally smaller — ideal for an individual serving — and usually savoury. They are a popular and convenient meal, perhaps to be eaten on a journey or at a rugby match. New Zealanders now consume some 68 million pies per year. Since 1997 local bakers have been able to compete for the Bakels New Zealand Supreme Pie Awards, with prizes given in 11 categories.

Tomato-sauce dispenser

A popular item found in New Zealand fish 'n' chip shops, where it once kept company with gingham table cloths and bottles of Worcestershire sauce, the red plastic tomato-sauce dispenser in the shape of a tomato has become a Kiwi icon.

Hokey-pokey ice cream

From the nineteenth century 'hokey pokey' was a term used for a type of ice cream sold by street vendors in parts of Britain and the United States, but in New Zealand it was originally the name of a tough form of toffee. In the 1940s the Meadowgold Ice Cream Company of Papatoetoe, Auckland, began making hokey-pokey ice cream, blending crunchy honeycomb toffee with vanilla ice cream. The flavour became popular and was produced by Tip Top (see page 243) from the early 1950s and it is, still, a top seller.

Jelly-Tip

The Jelly-Tip is a chocolate-coated ice cream on a stick with a tip of raspberry-flavoured jelly, developed and introduced by Tip Top in the 1950s. It remains popular today.

Anzac biscuits

New Zealand's favourite biscuit, the Anzac, has been baked in homes throughout this country and Australia from the early 1920s. University of Otago anthropologist Associate Professor Helen Leach has studied the evolution of the biscuit, and believes the earliest known recipe was published in Dunedin in 1921 — which slightly pre-dates the first known Australian recipe. During wartime, Kiwi and Aussie women would send batches of Anzac biscuits to their loved ones at the front. The recipe has no eggs, which were rationed, and their omission also meant the biscuits could travel the distance without going off.

There have been many recipe variations over the years. This Anzac biscuit recipe is from the 1940 Centennial Edition of the *New Zealand Women's Household Guide*:

¼ lb butter, ¾ cup sugar, ¾ cup flour, 1 cup coconut, pinch of salt, 1 cup oatina or rolled oats, 1 tablespoon golden syrup, 1 teaspoon soda dissolved in 1 tablespoon boiling water. Melt butter, add syrup, then soda dissolved in 1 tablespoon boiling water, beat for 1 minute, add the other ingredients. Put on a cold, greased slide. Bake till a nice brown top and bottom.

Eskimo pies

The eskimo pie is the oldest novelty ice cream made by Tip Top. It has its origins in Iowa, United States, in 1921 when a school teacher and candy-store owner combined ice cream with a candy bar, and named the product Eskimo Pie. In the 1930s it was promoted in New Zealand as an 'all-the-year-round confection — suitable for parties, dances, or as an after-dinner dessert'.

Bycroft biscuits

John Bycroft built a flour mill and biscuit factory in Onehunga in the mid-1850s. Later, he moved the business to Auckland's Shortland Street. In 1880 his large factory was producing about 70 different types of biscuit, including arrowroot, almond drops, cabin, chocolate, digestive, ginger and gingernut, macaroon, rusk, shrewsbury, vanilla wafer and water crackers. Early biscuits were sold from large tins with hinged lids, and were often stacked in front of the counter in grocery shops.

One of the more imaginative images on a New Zealand product was to be found on a Bycroft biscuit tin — it showed a boy holding a Bycroft biscuit tin on which was an image of a boy holding a Bycroft biscuit tin on which was an image of . . . and so on.

In 1982 Auckland writer Gordon McLauchlan recalled how his grandfather used the 'Bycrofts Biscuit Tin theory of the universe' to explain the idea of eternity. He pointed out that the pictures of the boy on the tin appeared to go on forever. However, the Bycrofts brand of biscuits did not and the biscuits went off the market in the 1970s.

Girl Guide biscuits

In 1957 the New Zealand Girl Guides Association began selling biscuits as a fundraiser. The plain biscuit became a national institution, with groups of uniformed girls selling packets door to door. In 1999, for the first time, it was available with a chocolate coating.

Lamington

A lamington is a cube of sponge cake coated with chocolate or raspberry-flavoured pink icing and rolled in dried coconut. It has been a popular treat in New Zealand since around 1915. However, it is named after Lord Lamington who was Governor of Queensland from 1895 to 1901 so it is likely to be an Australian invention.

Pavlova

The pavlova has been claimed as an Australian icon, but New Zealanders insist the meringue, cream and fruit dessert was invented on this side of the Tasman. What is not in doubt is that it was named after the Russian ballerina, Anna Pavlova, who toured New Zealand in 1926. The appearance of the dessert was inspired by her filmy white costume and pavlova recipes began appearing in New Zealand from 1927. By the 1960s the dessert was usually known simply as a pav. The Kiwi pav is typically topped with sliced kiwifruit.

Junket

Junket was a common dessert and party treat for young New Zealanders in the 1950s. It was made from rennet, an enzyme used in the cheese industry and extracted from the stomachs of bobby calves (see page 206). The cheese industry's main source of rennet was the New Zealand Co-op. Rennet Company at Eltham, in Taranaki. Established in 1916, it also made Renco, a liquid form of rennet used for junket. It became available in a range of flavours, but by the early 1960s junket had been largely replaced by rennet-free instant puddings that could be made in a flash.

Ice blocks

By the 1950s young New Zealanders were enjoying frozen blocks of articifially flavoured confection on sticks and the treats were known as ice blocks. The best known of these was the TT2, produced by Tip Top (see page 243). Today ice blocks are known as ice lollies in the United Kingdom and popsicles in the United States. They are available singly from dairies and petrol stations in a variety of flavours.

K-Bar

The K-Bar is a toffee bar, available in six flavours. It has a soft and chewy outside and a tough inside. It has long been popular in New Zealand and Australia, and is made by Whittaker's of Porirua. It is said the 'K' stands for Kwench, an alternative spelling of quench.

Jaffas

This small, round, orange sweet with a hard outside and a soft, chocolate centre first appeared in New Zealand in the early 1930s. It was named after the Jaffa orange from Israel. It gained iconic status in the days of wooden-floored movie theatres — people would roll the

Jaffas – the chocolate orange mouthful, inspired by a fruit from Israel, which became popular with young cinema-goers in New Zealand.

sweets down the sloping floor, causing a real racket! Perhaps that's what inspired the carpeting of cinemas?

Whittaker's chocolate

James Henry Whittaker, who worked in the chocolate business in Britain as a lad, arrived in New Zealand in 1890. Six years later he began making confectionery from his Christchurch home, and delivering it to customers by horse and van. In 1913 he went into partnership with his two sons and the Wellington-based J.H. Whittaker & Sons was formed. Business grew, and in 1931 the company was selected to supply its products to Woolworths' stores, recently established in New Zealand's four main cities. In 1992 the company began exporting to Australia, and four years later, to celebrate a century of business, Whittaker's launched a bigger version of its most popular product — the original peanut slab that had remained unchanged since 1952.

Queen Anne chocolates

Ernest Adams (see page 50) began producing Queen Anne chocolates and ice cream in Wellington in 1925 and were soon stocking bakeries and retail shops throughout New Zealand. By the 1930s over 60 varieties of Queen Anne chocolates were available from Adams Bruce and Queen Anne shops. Business grew but competition from supermarkets led to Queen Anne chocolates going out of production in 1976. In 1997 Sarah Adams, granddaughter of Ernest, successfully started making Queen Anne chocolates again, in time to produce a special 2lb limited-edition tin celebrating Queen Anne's seventy fifth jubilee in 2000.

Chocolate fish

A pink or white marshmallow fish covered in milk chocolate is one of New Zealand's favourite confections, and dates from at least the 1930s. So widely known and loved, the chocolate fish has long been used by New Zealanders to reward someone for doing a good deed or helping out or as a prize. 'You deserve a chocolate fish for that!'

Dining out

In 1961 New Zealanders were able to eat out and enjoy a quality dining experience at the country's first licensed restaurant, the Gourmet, in Auckland's Shortland Street. Before it become legal to drink wine with a restaurant meal in New Zealand, customers were known to smuggle bottles of wine and glasses in, under their coats. The Gourmet set the standard for the new approach to dining, with a refrigerated salad bar and a charcoal broiler for steaks and crayfish tails, waiters with white shirts and bowties, and toheroa soup on the menu.

Pie carts

Pie carts began appearing in towns and cities throughout New Zealand by the 1920s. They provided a basic menu, consisting mainly of pies (see page 40), and were popular with a range of customers — from colourful local characters and night owls to people needing a late meal after a dance or picture show. Pie carts began disappearing in the 1970s, following the rapid growth in the number and range of cafés and restaurants. However, one of the country's better-known pie carts is still in business — Auckland's White Lady. The White Lady began operating in Lower Shortland Street in 1950 and in 2006 was required to move around the corner to Commerce Street because of construction work.

Kai

The Maori wood for food or a meal — kai — was quickly adopted by early European settlers. In 1840 the explorer Edward J. Wakefield described seeing Maori 'kai or feasting'. Food gathered from the sea or lake is known as kaimoana.

Dinner

In earlier days in rural New Zealand the midday meal was usually referred to as dinner and was followed by a lighter evening meal known as tea. Dinner now refers to the main meal of the day, usually in the evening. Once upon a time, family members were forced to sit at the table until they had finished everything on their plate. Today dinner is most commonly eaten on laps in front of the TV.

Smoko

In the late 1800s when workers took regular morning and afternoon breaks they invariably enjoyed a cuppa and a cigarette. As a result, the foreman might advise of a break by shouting 'Smoke-ho!' or 'Smoke-o', which was shortened to 'Smoko'. The place where workers enjoy their breaks is still referred to as the smoko room or smoko shed in many workplaces.

Smoko was not restricted to the usual workplace. In 1886 an explorer in the southwest of the South Island described the difficulty of the terrain — crossing foaming mountain torrents, and clambering over fallen trees — and was reported as saying in the *Otago Witness*, 17 April 1886, that 'rests and smoke-ho's' were needed every 15 or 20 minutes.

Snarlers

A colloquial name for sausages and an essential item for the typical Kiwi barbie. In Australia sausages are also known as 'snags' and the British fondly call them 'bangers'.

New Zealand's original fast food, fish 'n' chips, was honoured when included in a series of Kiwiana postage stamps in 1994.

Fish 'n' chips

Fish 'n' chips are New Zealanders' favourite fast-food or takeaway meal. The fish is deep-fried in batter and wrapped in an insulating jacket of newsprint. Although it originated in the United Kingdom, Kiwis have put thir own stamp on the culinary tradition with many New Zealand fish-and-chip shops including kumara chips and whitebait and/or paua fritters on their menu. An alternative name for fish 'n' chips is shark and taties, acknowledging that the fish mostly used in this takeaway is in fact the rig shark, which is found in large numbers around New Zealand.

Takeaways

Now, what used to be an occasional treat is common fare for a lot of Kiwis, with many feeling takeaways are often cheaper (though less nutritious) than home cooking. A wide range of options is available all over the country, including foods of American, Chinese, Indian and Italian origin. In the United States such meals are described as takeouts, or food to go. New Zealanders prefer to call them takeaways — a term borrowed from Britain. Many takeaway operators also deliver to your door.

Ernest Adams

In 1920 English-born Ernest Adams and a New Zealand friend, Hugh Bruce, established the Adams Bruce bakery in Christchurch. The Ernest Adams name continues today in a range of home-style baking produced by Goodman Fielder. The Ernest Adams Christmas cake, pudding and fruit mince pies still dominate supermarket shelves.

A fine DROP

Tea

In 1937 New Zealand was introduced to Bushell's tea, which came from Australia and was advertised with this country's first radio jingle. It was also enthusiastically recommended by Aunt Daisy. Other tea brands that became national favourites were Choysa and Bell. In the early to mid-twentieth century, a cup of tea came to mean more than just a refreshment, it was also an opportunity for busy housewives to 'put their feet up' or catch up with neighbours for a chin-wag. A cup of tea was otherwise known as a cuppa.

Billies and jugs

Although allegedly originating in Australia, the billy (a tin can with a wire handle) was commonly used in New Zealand to boil water before the introduction of electricity to homes from 1916. This meant boiling a billy over an open-fired stove or range. Nowadays water is most likely to be boiled in an electric jug. The billy, or billy can, also refers to an enamelled or aluminum can used for holding milk.

Zip

Zip was the brand name for a small cylindrical water-heater that dates from the 1930s and was once found in all the tearooms, smoko rooms and motel units throughout New Zealand. It was usually located above the sink, and quickly provided boiling water for a cuppa or for washing dishes. It was operated with the pull of a string, and whistled when the water approached boiling point. It also had the annoying habit of squirting hot water out its top if not turned off in time. Although less common today, zip water heaters are still available.

In the New Zealand home a jug (usually electric) is boiled to provide water for a cup of tea, or cuppa. In earlier times a kettle was boiled on the stove.

Coffee

Coffee is the preferred daily (non-alcoholic) drink for an increasing number of New Zealanders. In recent years it has taken over from the tradition of drinking tea, which reflected this country's strong links with Britain. Coffee was available in New Zealand in the 1860s, and an early roaster was William Gregg, of Dunedin. However, the drink in the nineteenth century could be far from pure, for when coffee beans were not available they were replaced by chicory, a parsnip-like plant with a long taproot.

A fine DROP

Coffee drinking in New Zealand was revived in the 1940s when American servicemen introduced Nescafé, an instant coffee made by Nestlé. The idea caught on, and in 1960 Greggs offered an instant of its own. Coffee bars began to take over from milk bars and tea rooms, and in time they gave way to cafés. In the twenty-first century there is an increasing demand for baristas, those skilled in the art of producing a good cup of coffee.

Bottled water

The country's first aerated water factory opened in 1845, in Auckland's Eden Crescent, and operated there for 119 years until it became part of the Oasis Group of Companies. Today, with a population growing ever more health-conscious, bottled mineral and spring waters have become a multi-million-dollar industry in New Zealand alone. Many people, though, stand by the purity of 'good old tap water'.

Beer

Captain Cook brewed the first beer in this country, at Dusky Sound, on 27 March 1773. The drink was intended to improve the health of his sailors by preventing scurvy, and Cook recorded the brewing process:

We at first made our beer of a decoction of the spruce leaves; but, finding that this alone made it too astringent, we afterwards mixed with it an equal quantity of the tea plant (a name it obtained in my former voyage, from our using it as a tea then, as we also did now), which partly destroyed the astringency of the other, and made the beer exceedingly palatable, and esteemed by every one on board. We brewed it in the same manner as spruce beer, and the process is as follows. First make a strong decoction of the small branches of the spruce and tea-plants, by boiling them three or four hours, or until the bark will strip with ease from the branches; then take them out of the copper, and put in the proper quantity of molasses, ten gallons of which is sufficient to make a ton, or two hundred and forty gallons of beer. Let this mixture just boil, then put it into casks, and to it add an equal quantity of cold water, more or less according to the strength of the decoction, or your taste. When the whole is milk-warm, put in a little grounds of beer, or yeast if you have it, or anything else that will cause fermentation, and in a few days the beer will be fit to drink.

Any one who is in the least acquainted with spruce pines will find the tree which I have distinguished by that name. There are three sorts of it: that which has the smallest leaves and deepest colour is the sort we brewed with, but doubtless all three might safely serve that purpose.

— *Cook's Second Voyage towards the South Pole*, 4th ed. vol i, pages 99 and 101

Sixty-two years after Cook's 'decoction', the first brewery was established in New Zealand, at Kororareka — now Russell. By the 1900s there were breweries throughout the country.

Crates and bottles

In New Zealand, a crate is a particular type of container designed to carry a dozen beer bottles. Such open-topped wooden cases were made by ABC (Associated Bottling Company). The company was established in 1923 when New Zealand Glass Manufacturers started making beer bottles embossed with ABC at Penrose, South Auckland. ABC collected the empty bottles and rented them back to the breweries for refilling. Bottles have largely been replaced with canned drinks and stubbies.

Flagons and Jugs

The flagon was a glass container for beer, usually half a gallon (2.25 litres) — and, so, was also known as a half-g or half-gallon jar. It was particularly popular when the public bars of New Zealand were required to close at six o'clock (otherwise known as the 'six o'clock swill' — see page 245) and people would stock up with a flagon before heading home.

In the public bar a jug is a one-litre handled container, once made of glass but now made of plastic, used for selling beer to customers.

Wine

Wine was produced in New Zealand from the earliest days of European settlement, with the first vines planted by Samuel Marsden at a missionary station in the Bay of Islands in 1819. Until the 1950s, much of New Zealand's wine was regarded as inferior quality — and referred to as plonk. However, we've got better and we can now enjoy a range of top-quality locally produced wines, including chardonnay, sauvignon blanc, cabernet, merlot, pinot noir and pinot gris. Many New Zealand wines are now world class, particularly our sauvignon blancs and to a lesser extent our pinot noirs, and the wine industry has become a major export earner.

Cold Duck

This once popular New Zealand sparkling red wine had a name that was as unusual as its origins. Cold Duck, a sparkling red, apparently began in Germany when restaurant staff poured wine leftovers into a single bowl and named the mixture 'kalte Ende' — meaning 'cold ends'. This was mistaken for 'kalte Ente', which is German for 'cold duck'. Montana marketed a wine with this name in New Zealand in the 1970s at a time when local wine drinkers were less discerning. In 1997, to mark the twenty-fifth anniversary of Cold Duck, Montana released another 5000 cases. The company expected the drink to appeal to nostalgic wine drinkers, and it was described by one newspaper as 'Kiwiana regurgitated'. Even so it proved popular and quickly sold out.

Lindauer

Lindauer is a popular locally made sparkling wine which first appeared in 1981. It takes its name from the painter Gottfried Lindauer (1839–1926), who was born in Bohemia (now the Czech Republic) and came to New Zealand in 1873.

Soft drinks

Soft drinks, or fizzy drinks, have been manufactured in New Zealand for more than 150 years and during that period there have been some 560 bottlers, from Kaitaia to Invercargill. In the early days of the New Zealand soft-drink industry there was said to be a factory about every 20 miles — the limit a horse and cart delivery service could manage in a day! Eventually, local brands began to face competition from established overseas names, such as Schweppes, which arrived in Wellington in 1935, and Coca-Cola, which was introduced to New Zealand in 1939. Two of the best-known surviving local names are Foxton Fizz and Lemon & Paeroa.

Foxton Fizz

Foxton Fizz is produced in a factory in Foxton, Manawatu that has been operating since 1918. The company still uses glass bottles and the traditional range of flavours, including kola, orange, creaming soda, lime, lemonade, raspberry, cocktail, ginger beer, soda water and tonic water. The drinks are distributed throughout Manawatu, and can also be bought in Taranaki and Waikato. In 2008 the company shifted production to a modern factory in the Waikato town of Putaruru, and plans to return to Foxton at a later stage.

Lemon & Paeroa

Lemon & Paeroa — the soft drink that is famously 'world-famous in New Zealand' — began in a paddock in Paeroa. By the early 1900s local residents had discovered a spring that provided a refreshing drink. They began adding a slice or two of lemon to the mineral water for extra flavour. By about 1909 the water was being shipped in wooden casks to Auckland, where it was bottled for sale. But the cost of transportation, plus the increasing demand, led to the decision to analyse the natural mineral salts that gave the Paeroa water its distinctive flavour. An identical drink could then also be produced in Auckland, where it is still made. In 1972 Paeroa's famous drink was honoured when a 22 foot (6.7 metre) statue of an L&P bottle was unveiled at the end of the town's main street.

BYO & BYOG

In New Zealand a fully licensed restaurant can sell alcohol to diners. As is also the case in Australia, the United Kingdom and North America, a BYO (bring your own) restaurant is one with a different sort of licence that allows diners to take their own alcohol. Also, New Zealanders use the expression BYOG — bring your own grog (a word that originally referred to rum but became a general term for alcohol) — for parties and social occasions where guests are required to take their own alcohol.

Booze barn

A term coined to describe a hotel with a large bar that was able to quickly serve large amounts of beer. Thirsty drinkers would be likely to choose between popular brands mass-produced by the nation's two main breweries: DB (Dominion Breweries) Draught, which was said to reflect typical Kiwi values of strength, honesty, hard work and loyalty; and Lion Red, which was promoted in the 1970s as the 'Man's Brew'. Today the booze barn still exists, though the beer selection has broadened.

A fine DROP

Glad RAGS

Woollen clothing

Early European settlers needed clothes that were mostly practical and hard-wearing, reflecting their physical lifestyle. Following the successful introduction of sheep to New Zealand and the establishment of several woollen mills around the country, locally produced clothes were usually made of wool — it's hard-wearing and remains warm when wet, which makes it ideal for people who work outdoors.

By the end of the twentieth century, with the availability of cheaper imported clothes, the once common skill of hand-knitting was on the decline. But recent years have seen a revival of interest in the craft, and the production of more characterful clothes.

The black singlet

In the early 1900s working men in New Zealand began to wear a sleeveless woollen undergarment in serviceable black. Popular with bushmen, it became known as the bush singlet. By the 1930s it had also been adopted by shearers, farmers and most people who worked outdoors.

At first, New Zealand shearers knew their black singlet as the Jackie Howe, named in honour of a champion Australian shearer who wore one while working in this country in the 1890s. Workers in the frozen-meat industry also took to wearing the black singlet.

More recently, the black woollen singlet has gained an extra layer — of polypropylene — to draw moisture away from the skin of the wearer. At times, the lowly black singlet has even been a fashionable outer garment for women.

Swanndri

New Zealand's favourite outdoor shirt had its origins in 1913 when a New Plymouth mercer (a dealer in textiles), William Henry Broome, developed a rugged woollen water-resistant shirt ideal for bushworkers and farmers. He gave it the name Swanndri, due to the way water would run off it like water off a swan's back! These popular garments soon became an essential part of most New Zealanders' outdoor wardrobe — they were standard dress for farmers, fishermen, contractors, and industrial and power-supply workers. By 1994 the bush shirt — also known as a swannie — had become accepted as part of the national wardrobe. The most popular styles have always been olive green and Swanndri's distinctive red and black plaid (pictured right). In 2006 Swanndri commissioned leading fashion designer Karen Walker to design a range of clothing for them.

Walk shorts & walk socks

During the 1960s walk shorts became popular summer wear among New Zealand males. It was an idea that dated back to the lighter uniforms worn in hotter climates by Second World War servicemen. The shorts were made mostly in synthetic materials and had a permanent crease down the front and back of each leg. They were worn with thick and nearly knee-high socks known as walk socks and sometimes sandals and a woollen cardigan too. Walk shorts and socks were popular until the end of the 1970s — they were considered acceptably tidy and neat for workers in government departments.

The hard-wearing Swanndri shirt, an essential part of the national wardrobe.

Glad RAGS 63

Stubbies

In 1972 Australian males were introduced to a new type of ultra-short shorts known as stubbies. They claimed to be 'the shortest legs this side of decency' and became something of a national institution. Before long these casual shorts were also available in New Zealand.

Canterbury Clothing

The world's largest dedicated rugby-clothing company had its origins in 1880 when Christchurch couple Alfred and Sarah Rudkin began a home industry making men's socks and cardigans. In 1904 they merged with two Timaru woollen mill owners, John Lane and Pringle Walker, and Lane Walker Rudkin was formed. The company made army uniforms during the First World War, and produced playing kit for the All Blacks, an association that would last for 73 years until the New Zealand Rugby Union switched sides and awarded the contract to Adidas. In April 2009, after more than 125 years of making clothes for New Zealanders and markets overseas, Lane Walker Rudkin was placed in receivership.

Lemon squeezer

The lemon squeezer is a wide-brimmed felt hat long associated with the New Zealand Army. It got its popular name from the four dents on its pointed crown. A form of this hat was first worn by New Zealanders serving in the Boer War (1899–1902), and it was generally adopted during the First World War. Although it was replaced in 1960 — members of the New Zealand Army Corps now wear berets — the lemon squeezer is still worn by soldiers for ceremonial duties.

Togs

The word togs — from the Latin *toga* — was used in New Zealand from the early 1900s to descibe clothes needed for a special occasion or event, such as playing sport. At some point New Zealanders began to refer to bathing togs and swimming togs, and later shortened it to just 'togs' — the only common use of the word today. The word is exclusively native to New Zealand and if you use the term anywhere overseas, you're likely to receive some slightly perplexed looks.

Gumboots

In England Wellingtons, or wellies, are protective footwear named after the Duke of Wellington. Perhaps because New Zealand had already named its capital after the Duke, the footwear became known here as gumboots. The name is derived from gum Arabic — a rubbery substance exuded by trees. At first, gumboots were imported into New Zealand in the late nineteenth century. The first locally made gumboots were the Marathon brand, by Skellerup, made in Christchurch in 1943. For economic reasons, Skellerup moved production offshore in the late 1970s, but the company's current range of gumboots includes the Perth — the original tall farm boot — and the mid-calf length Red Band, introduced in 1958.

The gumboot has been celebrated in song by Fred Dagg. Taihape proclaims itself New Zealand's Gumboot Capital and since 1985 has hosted an annual festival that includes gumboot throwing (using a man's long size-8 Perth boot), decorated gumboots and a Fred Dagg look-alike competition. 'Gumboot tea' is a term used to decribe stock-standard black tea, i.e. nothing fancy.

Glad RAGS

Jandals

The casual footwear known in New Zealand as the Jandal goes by other names overseas: flip-flops in England and the United States, thongs in Australia, and baffies in Scotland. Whatever the name, they evolved from the traditional Japanese shoe with a wooden or woven sole. The idea was taken back to the United States by servicemen who had been in Japan during the Second World War, while Australia was introduced to it in 1956 by the Japanese swimming team that competed at the Melbourne Olympic Games. The following year an Auckland businessman, Morris Yock, returned from a visit to Asia and brought the idea to New Zealand. He went into production, and named his new footwear Jandal — from 'Japanese sandal'. The first Jandals were made of brown and white rubber, and production was later taken over by Skellerup Industries of Christchurch. Over half a century later, the original Jandal remains popular with New Zealanders, but it now faces competition from imported look-alikes and other inexpensive casual footwear.

Sandshoes

The casual rubber-soled footwear is known in other countries as the tennis shoe. One of this country's biggest and earliest brands of sandshoe was Marathon, which began in 1939 and was manufactured by Skellerup Industries of Christchurch.

Roman sandals

In the nineteenth century, New Zealanders' feet were likely to be secure inside sturdy boots. During the Second World War, lighter

New Zealand's favourite casual footwear, the Jandal, introduced in the late 1950s and seen here in its most popular colour scheme of blue and white.

footwear was developed for service personnel in warmer climates, and this led to sandals for civilian use becoming popular back in New Zealand. The most popular were Roman sandals, available in a range of colours and with adjustable straps to allow for growing feet.

The main manufacturer of New Zealand's Roman sandals, established in 1949 and still going strong, is Douglas Sandals Ltd, of Auckland. The company estimates that some 10 per cent of all New Zealanders were wearing Roman sandals in the 1970s, and the current range of Roman sandals includes five colours — black, brown, blue, red and green. Today the primary market is the school uniform-wearing type.

Glad RAGS

Kaydee sandals

In the 1950s two returned servicemen, Mick Kyne and Mervyn Devine, started the Kaydee footwear company in Auckland — the name was inspired by their own surnames. Their best-known product was a plastic sandal, known as the Kaydee sandal which, was produced by Plastic Products in Hamilton. Despite having a tendency to skid on certain surfaces, the sandals proved popular due to their durability and waterproof nature, especially in the upper North Island. At their peak they sold 250,000 pairs of sandals a year.

Ugg boots

Several people claim to have invented uggs. One is Adelaide surfer John Arnold who came up with the idea in 1965, but another Australian, surfer Shane Steadman, registered the name 'ugg' (a slang derivative of 'ugly') and begin selling boots of that name in 1971. Before long, ugg boots were popular in New Zealand.

The idea is said to date back to when Australian and New Zealand shearers wrapped sheepskin around their feet to keep warm. Sheepskin boots were also popular with aviators in the First and Second World Wars, and the thermal properties of the material were also recognised by surfers.

Short back and sides

The hairstyle popular with mainstream New Zealand males until at least the 1960s was known as the 'short back and sides'. It was celebrated by Peter Cape in his 1958 song 'Down the Hall on a Saturday Night'.

Op-shop chic

Opportunity shops, selling donated used goods — mostly clothing — to raise money for charity, were established in New Zealand by at least the 1930s. By the 1990s, wearing 'retro' second-hand clothing became popular amongst some young people (although, ironically, they considered themselves 'alternative' to what was popular or mainstream). About that time second-hand shops became known as op shops (short for opportunity shops). The name Opshop has also been adopted by a popular rock group from Christchurch.

Scarfies

Around 1990, university students in Dunedin developed a distinctive look that gets its name from the neckwear needed in the colder southern climate. The term became more widely recognised with the 1999 film *Scarfies* — directed by Robert Sarkies, and written by Robert and Duncan Sarkies — which told of the misadventures of five Dunedin flatmates.

Westies

Westies are associated with the northwestern suburbs of Auckland. However, it is not an original New Zealand term — it has also been used in connection with certain suburbs in the west of Sydney, Australia, from about 1977. In Auckland, the term Westie implies a certain dress sense, which for men is likely to include a black T-shirt and black denim jeans. It is also used to describe a subculture with a strong interest in cars. In 2005 the lifestyle went under the spotlight in a popular black-comedy television series, *Outrageous Fortune*, which featured a family with the surname West who were described as 'a one-family crime wave'. *Outrageous Fortune* began its fifth series in June 2009.

Bodgies and widgies

In the mid-1950s New Zealanders began to discover a new type of young male labelled the bodgie. He was known to frequent milk bars, enjoy riding motorcycles, and he was easily recognised by his swept back hair and denim jeans. His female associates, who had similar habits and appearance, were known as widgies.

In 1958 a New Zealand psychologist wrote a small book on the subject of the bodgie and subtitled it: 'A study in abnormal psychology'. He provided a number of alternative names for bodgies and widgies and their kind, including yahoos, larrikins, hooligans and yobs. He described them as '[the] social end-products of two devastating wars and the possible victims of a third'.

—*The Bodgie: A Study in Abnormal Psychology*, A.E. Manning, A.H. & A.W. Reed, Wellington, 1958

Bonzer

The expression bonzer, meaning something large and impressive, first appeared in both Australia and New Zealand in the early 1900s. In 1902 a New Zealand newspaper reported that an American guest at the forthcoming coronation of Edward VII would be wearing a dress that cost £250,000, and so she must be what the boys call a 'bonzer'. Today the expression is more commonly evident in Aussie vernacular as an exclamation of approval or delight.

Five bodgies and a widgie, seen as a social problem in New Zealand in the 1950s, drawn by Wanganui-born artist Dennis K. Turner.

Glad RAGS 71

Skiting

The term skiting — meaning boasting or showing off — was in use in Australia by the 1850s, and so came across to New Zealand. In 1880 a boot and shoemaker in Princes Street, Hawera, south Taranaki, advertised his wares with the following ditty:

When Noble snobs do blow and skite
About their work and watertights,
Just at their boots take a peep —
You then will rush to Princes street.

— *Hawera & Normanby Star*, 1 May 1880

Strides

In New Zealand and Australia, men's trousers were once referred to as strides. The likely lad in Peter Cape's 1958 song 'Down the Hall on a Saturday Night' teams a brown sports coat with a pair of grey strides.

At the CHALKFACE

Varsity

The term varsity, as an abbreviation for university, had reached New Zealand from Britain by the 1860s. At first the term was used mostly in relation to sport, as in an 1877 report on a cricket match in Dunedin when Paramor and Hewat 'batted well for Varsity'. A century later varsity had become the usual New Zealand term for university in general, but the even shorter uni —- adopted from our cousins across the Tasman — has become more common in recent times.

Secondary school

New Zealand's first post-primary or secondary schools offered mostly academic subjects, but from 1905 technical high schools provided courses in practical subjects. Over the years the country's schools have acquired different names, and so were known variously as grammar schools, high schools, colleges, technical high schools and technical colleges.

Intermediate school

New Zealand's first intermediate school was Kowhai Intermediate, in Kingsland, Auckland. It opened in October 1922 to cater for form one to three pupils and, at first, it was known as Kowhai Junior High School. By 1944 there were 12 intermediate schools in the country. The late 1950s saw the building of a large number of intermediate schools to cope with pupils born after the Second World War.

Primary school

Since 1877, New Zealand children have been legally obliged to attend primary school once they reach the age of six. Eligibility is generally decided by zoning (whether the child lives in a school's designated area). Children spend six years at primary school before they move on to intermediate.

Normal school

Normal schools began in France in the nineteenth century and were educational facilities used for training student teachers. In New Zealand some primary schools are called 'normal' schools, which means they are linked with a college of education — previously known as a teachers' training college.

Open-air classroom

The open-air classroom with a verandah and a large number of windows became a feature of New Zealand schools in the mid-1900s as the Plunket Society (see page 18) promoted the benefits of fresh air and sunshine. In 1924 Fendalton School, in Christchurch, became the first school in the country to have a new classroom built this way. On sunny days, large glass sliding doors could be opened to let sunshine and fresh air into the classroom. Weather permitting, children might also be able to carry their desk and chair outside to work.

Kohanga reo

The system of kohanga reo — language nests — to provide educational and cultural opportunities for pre-school Maori children began in 1982, near Wellington. Teaching at kohanga reo is entirely in the Maori language. By 1994 the country had 800 kohanga reo catering for 14,000 children, and there are now believed to have been about 60,000 'graduates' of the movement.

Correspondence School

The Correspondence School was established in 1922 to provide lessons to New Zealand children living in isolated areas and others unable, for whatever reason, to attend their local school. The school began with some 100 primary children, providing lessons sent through the post. The school had two principals, in charge of the primary and post-primary departments.

In 1937 the Correspondence School began regular radio broadcasts, and in 1949 it offered a course in Maori — the first of its kind. The school moved into its present home in Thorndon, Wellington, in 1979, and it now has 13,000 students on its roll at any one time, making it the largest school in the country.

School bus and walking school bus

From 1924 the school bus service brought Kiwi children to school from outlying districts and was provided free. Those who lived closer, and could walk or ride bikes, might have been referred to as 'townies' by contrast.

Over the last few decades many New Zealand children have been driven to school instead of walking and cycling. To get children back into walking, the English initiative of the walking school bus was introduced to New Zealand cities in 1999. Among other things, it encourages physical activity, raises children's awareness of their neighbourhood and reduces the number of cars on the road. In Auckland in 2007 there were about 4000 children at 100 different schools taking part in 230 walking school bus routes.

Proficiency Examination

Until 1937 young New Zealanders were required to pass the Proficiency Examination before they could begin secondary schooling. The examination had been introduced in 1899 and passing it was known as 'getting one's proficiency'.

Matriculation

In order to go to university people had to pass an examination known as the Matriculation. Passing was commonly referred to as 'getting Matric'.

School Certificate

New Zealand's School Certificate examination — later shortened to School Cert or just School C — was introduced in 1934 as a school-leaving qualification. In 1945 it became the only Form Five award and was awarded for the aggregate results in English and three other subjects — candidates were required to gain 200 marks out of a total of 400 and it was necessary to gain at least 50 marks in English. After nearly 70 years' service, School C began to be phased out in 2002 with the introduction of NCEA — the National Certificate of Educational Achievement— Level 1.

University Entrance

University Entrance — known simply as UE — was established in the late 1920s to allow entry to a New Zealand university. It was awarded by accrediting — a form of internal assessment at approved schools — or by examination. It was replaced in 1986 with the fully internally assessed Six Form Certificate, which was, in turn, replaced in 2003 with NCEA Level 2.

Bursary

The University Bursaries Examination — usually referred to simply as Bursary — began in 1966. Students sat it in their last year of school — Form Seven, or Upper-sixth Form, now known as Year 13. Depending on marks, candidates were awarded an A or B bursary, which provided fees and allowances for study at university. The examination was abolished in 2003, and the following year it was replaced by NCEA Level 3.

Military drill

New Zealand secondary school boys were once required to undertake compulsory cadet service, or military drill. It was first introduced at Dunedin High School, in 1864, and was taken up by other schools during the Boer War (1899–1902). Cadet numbers reached a high point during the First World War, and then began to decline in the 1930s. In the 1960s a number of schools withdrew from the scheme. There were further changes, such as allowing girls to join in 1978. For many New Zealand males, school cadets meant uncomfortable khaki uniforms — known as sandpaper suits.

School dental clinics

The generally poor state of New Zealanders' teeth led to the founding of the School Dental Service in 1921. In the 1950s and 1960s New Zealand children often referred to the school dental clinic as 'the murder house'. One of the least appealing aspects of a visit to the clinic in the early days was the slow grind of the treadle drill, which the nurse operated by foot. By 2001 a little less than half of the primary and intermediate schools around the country had dental clinics on site. The rest were served by mobile clinics and the School Dental Service was providing care for more than 500,000 children, ranging from pre-schoolers to intermediate age.

Health camps and health stamps

In 1919 Dr Elizabeth Gunn, a school medical officer at Wanganui, organised a summer camp for children who were not properly nourished. Other camps followed and the first permanent health camp was established at Otaki in 1932. Funds were raised by donation and, from 1929, the sale of health stamps. The first health stamps cost 2d (twopence) — 1d (a penny) for postage and 1d for health camps. The second set of health stamps, issued in 1930, depicted a smiling young New Zealander and are now the highly sought after 'Red Boy' and 'Blue Boy'. Today health camps are used for children with a wide range of problems, including behavioural and emotional difficulties. There are currently seven camps, caring for about 4000 children each year.

Janet and John

In the 1950s New Zealand schoolchildren were taught to read with the *Janet and John* series of stories. They were originally written by a New Zealand teacher living in England, but first published and used in the United States. They then appeared in the United Kingdom and proved extremely popular, and only later were introduced to New Zealand. They had a simple and repetitive style, designed to help young readers develop a quick and reasonable vocabulary. But by the end of the 1950s the books were considered too limiting and were replaced.

Native Animals of New Zealand

The familiar orange-and-black covered guide book first appeared in 1947. It was written and illustrated by A.W.B. Powell, assistant director at the Auckland War Memorial Museum, who produced over 400 exquisite line drawings of New Zealand's native animals — from tapeworms to sperm whales. The book was reprinted within three months and remained in print for the next 60 years. In 1998 it underwent a major update with a new cover and a slight name change to *Powell's Native Animals of New Zealand*. It is still in print today.

School Journal

In 1907 the Department of Education produced the first copy of the *New Zealand School Journal*, which became familiar to generations

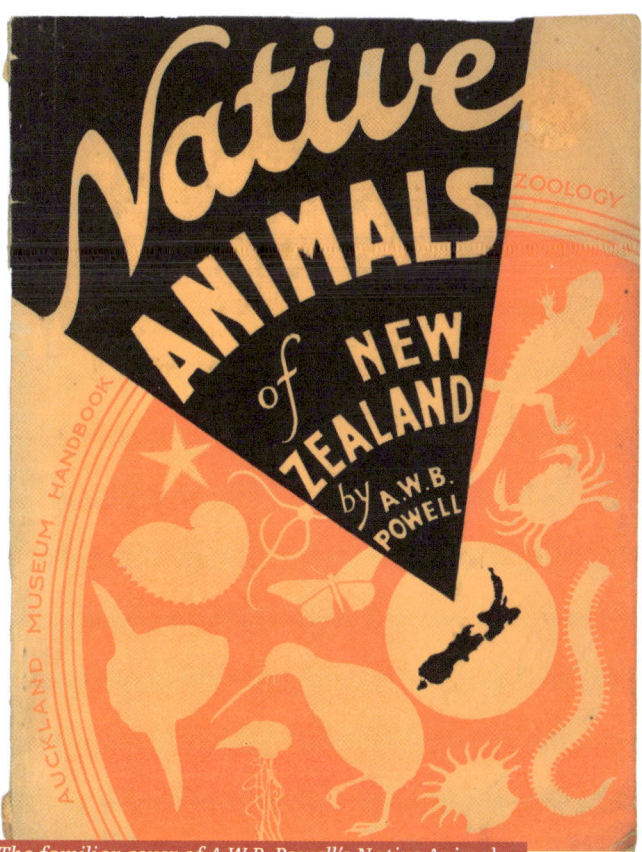

The familiar cover of A.W.B. Powell's Native Animals of New Zealand, *which was first published in 1947.*

At the CHALKFACE 81

of this country's schoolchildren. It began as a slender black-and-white publication, but by the 1950s had grown more substantial and included a colour cover. Over the years it has included the work of well-known New Zealand writers such as James K. Baxter, Janet Frame and Margaret Mahy, and illustrators such as Russell Clark, E. Mervyn Taylor and Rita Angus.

The centenary of the publication was marked in 2007 with an exhibition, 'A Nest of Singing Birds: 100 Years of the *New Zealand School Journal*', at the National Library, Wellington, and the publication of a book of the same name, by Gregory O'Brien. The *School Journal* is now published by Learning Media for the Ministry of Education and it is distributed free to all schools in New Zealand, and to schools in the South Pacific and Papua New Guinea. As well as being a publication children can read for their own interest, the *School Journal* is used as a teaching resource across the curriculum, including social studies and science.

Calf club

Due to the high number of farming families in New Zealand, most rural children naturally took an interest in young animals. This was encouraged in the early 1900s by annual events known as 'calf club', when children exhibited pet animals at their schools. Although known as calf club, it included other animals such as lambs and goats. Today fewer children have access to farm animals, but the annual events — now known in some areas as calf day, pet day or agriculture day — are still held in a large number of schools around New Zealand. Pet calves and lambs — and now dogs, cats, rabbits (which had earlier been classed as noxious pests and were not allowed to be kept as pets) and

This colourful cover of a 1965 School Journal *was designed by Jill McDonald. The publication began in 1907, when it was strictly black and white.*

At the CHALKFACE

guinea pigs — are paraded and can win prizes for their presentation and behaviour. Proud owners of calves and lambs may also be able to exhibit their pets at the local A&P Show (see page 225).

Sand saucer

The sand saucer — an arrangement of flower petals on a saucer filled with sand — has long been a popular section in school calf-day competitions. At the annual calf club and flower show held by the Kokopu School, in Whangarei, in October 2008, children were invited to enter competitions for sand saucers as well as flower arrangements in a vase, photo frames decorated with buttons and beads, vegetable animals, dinosaur-scapes and 'thingamajigs' — gadgets made from metal, mesh, driftwood and plastic.

Play-lunch

Play-lunch is a snack — perhaps an apple or sandwich — taken to school to eat during the mid-morning interval or playtime.

School milk

From 1937 to 1967 young New Zealanders were given a free half-pint bottle of milk at school every morning. This scheme was introduced to help children who had become undernourished during the Depression. For the next 30 years, the metal crates full of bottles were carried into the classroom by official milk monitors, who were also responsible for collecting up the empties after the drinking session.

Young New Zealanders busy at their mid-morning ritual, drinking their free half-pint of milk.

At the CHALKFACE 85

Jungle gym

The jungle gym was once a popular feature of the New Zealand primary-school playground. The metal climbing and swinging frame was also known as monkey bars.

Tall poppy

A tall poppy is someone who excels, or stands out from the crowd. It is a term commonly used in New Zealand and Australia and is usually used when referring to 'tall poppy syndrome' — an unfortunate willingness on the part of the average Antipodean to criticise or 'knock' someone who is a high achiever.

Prefabs

In 1840 a prefabricated mansion was shipped from England to Auckland, for use by Governor William Hobson as New Zealand's first government house. Now the term prefab refers to a portable classroom that can be moved from one school to another, as school rolls and needs for space change.

Crouch, Touch, ENGAGE

Rugby

Rugby began here in the 1870s and by the early 1880s New Zealand had hosted a team from New South Wales and made a return tour there. The first union was founded in Canterbury in 1879, followed soon afterwards by Wellington, Otago and Auckland, and the New Zealand Rugby Union began in 1892. In 1904 the provinces began competing for the Ranfurly Shield (see page 91), and in 1905–06 the first national team to be known as the All Blacks toured the United Kingdom, France and North America. The alleged importance of our 'national game' was reflected in the title of a song, by Rod Derrett, in the mid-1960s — *Rugby, Racing and Beer*. Rugby is still by far the nation's favourite sport.

All Blacks

The first national rugby team to be known as All Blacks toured the United Kingdom, France and North America in 1905–06. The origin of the name is believed to relate to a mistake in an English newspaper headline that changed All Backs — a reference to their speed — to All Blacks. The name stuck and the black uniform followed shortly after. During that tour the All Blacks lost only one game — a controversial loss to Wales and their first test match loss. Their resulting tour record was described as 'the most wonderful achievement in the annals of sport'.

The All Blacks played South Africa for the first time in 1921. They won, but it was another 35 years before they were able to win a test series against the Springboks. In all, and up until June 2008, the All Blacks had a success rate of nearly 75 per cent.

All Black halfback Jon Preston eludes a balletic opponent during a match against the British Lions in 1993.

Crouch, touch, ENGAGE 89

The total number of individuals who have played for the All Blacks passed the 1000 mark in 2001. To this day the top points scorer for the All Blacks is Andrew Mehrtens, who has tallied up a total of 967 points.

Well-known All Blacks include Donald Barry Clarke, who was born in 1933 and wore the jersey from 1956 to 1964. Because of his remarkable ability to kick goals he was known as The Boot. He first played for his province, Waikato, in 1951 at the age of 17, and five years later was selected for the All Blacks. During his career as an All Black Clarke scored 781 points, a record that was unbroken for the next 24 years. He died in 2002.

Perhaps the best known All Black and most famous rugby player in the world has been Colin Meads, who played a record 133 games for the team — 55 of which were test matches. Born in Cambridge in 1936, Meads was a lock and loose forward, and played for the All Blacks from 1957 to 1971, including four times as captain. He was a player of great strength — hence his nickname, Pinetree. In 1999 a New Zealand rugby publication proclaimed him New Zealand Player of the Century, and in the New Year Honours list of 2001 he was named a New Zealand Companion of Merit.

1981 Springbok tour

The 1981 Springbok tour of New Zealand was embroiled in violent protest and political debate concerning the ethics of playing against a team from apartheid-ruled South Africa.

Five-eighths

In the New Zealand rugby team the positions of fly half and inside centre are usually known as first five-eighth or first five and second five-eighth or second five. The names came about following a suggestion that a player located between the halfback and the three-quarter line would, mathematically speaking, be a five-eighth.

Ranfurly Shield

From 1897 to 1904, the Earl of Ranfurly was the fifteenth Governor of New Zealand — a role that is now known as Governor-General. In 1902 His Excellency presented the New Zealand Rugby Union with its premier rugby trophy for the newly established interprovincial competition. The Ranfurly Shield was first presented to Auckland — the team that had the best record for 1902. The first competition for the shield was held in 1904 — Wellington challenged successfully. The record for the longest run of successful defences of the shield is 61, set by Auckland from 1985 to 1993. A popular nickname for the shield is the 'log of wood'.

Rugby league

The New Zealand Warriors are a professional rugby league team based at Mount Smart Stadium in Auckland. Founded in 1995, they were originally known as the Auckland Warriors. They compete in Australasia's top rugby league competition — the National Rugby League premiership or NFL. The Warriors' most successful season to date was 2002 when they played in the grand final of the NFL, losing to the Sydney Roosters.

Crouch, touch, ENGAGE

Soccer

The Football Association was formed in the United Kingdom in 1863 and the term 'association football' was introduced to distinguish the 'round ball game' from rugby. It is believed the word soccer was an abbreviation of association. Interestingly, while Britain came to regard the game as 'football', it is now known as soccer in the United States, Australia and, of course, New Zealand. Soccer is the most popular sport in the world, although it has never been the major winter code in New Zealand. Soccer in this country is administered by New Zealand Football, and the national men's team is known as the All Whites.

Black Caps

New Zealand's national cricket team has played on the international stage since 1896. It made its first overseas tour — to Australia — in 1898 and in the 1929–30 season, the team played its first test match — against England at Christchurch. However, it was not until 1955–56 that it won a test, against the West Indies at Eden Park, Auckland. The New Zealand cricket team became known as the Black Caps in January 1998 — the name was chosen by running a competition.

Underarm bowling

On 1 February 1981, at the Melbourne Cricket Ground, the New Zealand team needed to score six runs from the last ball to tie the game. To prevent this, Australian captain Greg Chappell ordered his younger brother Trevor to bowl underarm. It was impossible to hit a ball delivered that way any distance, so New Zealand batsman Brian

McKechnie blocked it as it rolled towards him and then threw his bat down in disgust. New Zealand Prime Minister Robert Muldoon described Chappell's unsporting act as 'The most disgusting incident I can recall in the history of cricket'. Others have referred to that date, 1 February 1981, as 'a day of infamy' and others claimed the incident 'had become part of what was unique between the two countries'.

Yachting

New Zealanders have enjoyed the sport of yachting, or sailing, since the earliest days of European settlement. The first races for yachts were held on Auckland's Waitemata Harbour on 18 September 1840, when the settlement replaced Russell as the capital of the colony. The Auckland Anniversary Day Regatta has been held every year since on the Monday closest to 29 January — apart from 1900 when it was cancelled due to the war in South Africa. It has often been described as 'the biggest one-day regatta in the world'.

Yacht clubs were formed in the four main centres in the late nineteenth century. New Zealanders have done well at international regattas in many different classes of boat and have even challenged, on several occasions, for yachting's biggest prize — the America's Cup (see page 94).

Peter Blake is New Zealand's best-known yachtsman. Born in 1949, he grew up in Bayswater, a seaside suburb on Auckland's North Shore, where he began racing boats at the age of eight. He took part in four Whitbread round-the-world races, which he won with *Steinlager* in 1989–90. In 1992 he managed New Zealand's challenge for the

America's Cup and, three years later, did it again with Team New Zealand's *Black Magic* winning the cup. During this campaign Peter Blake's red socks became a patriotic symbol. In 1995 he was knighted for services to yachting. In 2000 Sir Peter Blake once again led Team New Zealand in its successful defence of the America's Cup.

During 2001 he led expeditions to Antarctica and the Amazon, but in December that year he was murdered by pirates in Brazil, South America. Sir Peter was buried in a churchyard on the south coast of England, where he had lived.

P-class

Older New Zealand sailors are likely to have first learned to sail in a P-class, the smallest competitive class of yacht. Designed by Harry Highet, a keen yachtsman and a draughtsman in the Public Works Department in Whangarei, the first P-class was launched on New Year's Day, 1920, at Onerahi Bay, just 10 kilometres from the centre of Whangarei. The new yacht proved popular, and within a few years a competitive class was formed — races continue today under the control of the Tauranga Yacht Club. In recent years the P-class has lost ground to another small class designed for young yachtsmen, the Optimist.

America's Cup

New Zealand's first challenge for the cup in KZ7 — known as *Kiwi Magic* — was unsuccessful at Fremantle in 1987. The following year businessman Michael Fay challenged the San Diego Yacht Club with a huge monohull, KZ1, but was also

Sir Peter Blake on laundry duty, hanging out the famous lucky red socks associated with Team New Zealand's victorious America's Cup campaign in 1995.

Crouch, touch, ENGAGE

unsuccessful. Then in 1995, in a major campaign led by Sir Peter Blake and his famously lucky red socks, the Russell Coutts-helmed *Black Magic* beat Dennis Conner's *Young America* in five successive races and commentator Peter Montgomery famously declared: 'America's Cup is now New Zealand's Cup'.

In 2000 Team New Zealand's yacht NZL82 beat the Italian syndicate — Prada's *Luna Rossa* — in Auckland to retain the America's Cup, but three years later it lost to Swiss challenger *Alinghi*, which was skippered by Russell Coutts.

Surf lifesaving

This country is surrounded by the sea, and in the late 1800s New Zealanders were encouraged to swim in the sea for the good of their health. It became a popular pastime, but there was always the issue of safety. The surf lifesaving movement began in New South Wales, Australia, and was brought across to New Zealand soon after. The first surf lifesaving clubs began here around 1910 at New Brighton in Christchurch and Lyall Bay in Wellington. Competition between provincial teams dates from 1915 and by the mid-1960s more than 40 teams were competing for over 30 titles. There are now 71 clubs around the country, from Ahipara in the far north to Oreti in the deep south. The New Zealand Surf Lifesaving Association was formed in 1932.

Jogging and running

Running at a leisurely rather than competitive pace to increase fitness was first promoted by New Zealand athletics coach Arthur Lydiard, who trained such runners as Peter Snell and Murray

Halberg. Lydiard started a joggers' group in Auckland and by the early 1960s the idea had spread to the United States. It rapidly went on to become a worldwide craze. Arthur Lydiard was born in Auckland in 1917. He was awarded an OBE in 1962 and made a member of the Order of New Zealand in 1990. He died in 2004.

Peter Snell was born in 1938 and went on to become one of the best middle-distance runners of all time. He was virtually unknown when he burst onto the scene and won the 800 metres at the Rome Olympics in 1960. Later that same day fellow New Zealander Murray Halberg also won a gold medal in the 5000 metres. At the 1964 Tokyo Olympics Snell won the 800- and 1500-metre races — the first in a record time. He had remarkable finishing speed, and in 1964 he improved on his own world record for the mile. Snell retired from athletics a year later. He is now an acknowledged world expert in the areas of human ageing, exercise and nutrition.

Twenty-one years after Roger Bannister became the first person to run a mile under four minutes, the next major barrier — three minutes and 50 seconds — was broken by a New Zealander. Auckland-born John Walker ran a mile in three minutes and 49.4 seconds in Goteborg, Sweden, on 12 August 1975. The following year he won the gold medal for the 1500 metres at the Montreal Olympics. Walker was also the first to run 100 sub-four-minute miles. In 2009 he was knighted for his services to sport and the community and became Sir John Walker.

Horse racing

The horse was introduced to New Zealand by missionary Samuel Marsden in 1814 and the animal became a vital form of transport in the young colony. Horse racing also became a feature of the early settlements. The first race meeting was held at Te Aro, Wellington, on 22 January 1841, and was followed by one at Epsom, Auckland, on 5 January 1842. Soon there were few boroughs in New Zealand without their own racecourse. The number of racing clubs has since reduced, and there are now 65 licensed racing or jockey clubs in New Zealand with 52 racecourses from Whangarei to Invercargill.

Best Bets

Best Bets is a small pocket-sized magazine that appears twice weekly and covers horse racing — gallops and trotting — and greyhound racing in New Zealand. It has the distinction of being incorporated in a 1980 painting, *No Son of Mine Goes to University*, by Canterbury artist Trevor Moffitt.

TAB

The TAB — Totalisator Agency Board — was established in 1949 when a law was passed that allowed gamblers to make off-course — away from the racecourse — bets on horse races. Previously, the only legal betting on horse races could be done at a racecourse. The TAB opened agencies throughout New Zealand and now takes bets on the outcome of other national and international sports, such as cricket, rugby and tennis, as well as horse racing.

A totalisator — known as a tote — is a device which records bets and calculates dividends, work which was previously done by clerks. The first automatic totalisator was invented by an Australian, George Julius, but New Zealand was first to accept the new system when one of Julius's machines was installed at Auckland's Ellerslie Racecourse in 1913. In recent years totalisators have been replaced by computers.

Desert Gold

Desert Gold was an outstanding New Zealand racehorse whose career began in 1914 and included a sequence of 19 successive wins. She also competed across the Tasman, beating the best Australian horses. The name Desert Gold may have been inspired by the title of a 1913 adventure novel written by American Zane Grey. A well-known brand of cigarettes (see Smoking page 128) was named after this horse, with the tin carrying an image of it.

Phar Lap

Phar Lap was a galloper and some say he was the best racehorse ever produced in New Zealand. His name means 'lightning flash' in Singhalese. In 1928 he was taken to race in Australia, winning the 1930 Melbourne Cup and going on to become a record stake-winner. Phar Lap was then taken to Mexico, where he won America's richest race, but less than three weeks later he died. It now appears the horse was poisoned by chemicals his trainer had been using as tonics and ointments. New Zealand-born Phar Lap was known as 'Big Red', and Australians also consider him an icon of their country. In death Phar Lap has been well distributed: his hide is in the Museum

A well-trained New Zealand marching team steps out.

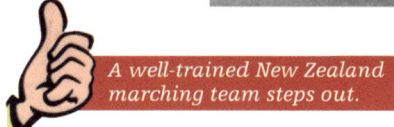

of Melbourne, his heart is in the National Museum of Australia in Canberra, and his skeleton remains in Te Papa Tongarewa, Museum of New Zealand.

Crikey!

Cardigan Bay

One of New Zealand's most famous racehorses, Cardigan Bay was the first pacer in the world to win a million dollars. The horse was born in Southland in 1956 and enjoyed a highly successful career in New Zealand and Australia before racing in the United States. Cardigan Bay returned to New Zealand in 1970 for a well-earned retirement.

Marching

Marching in formation as a competitive sport began in New Zealand during the Depression of the 1930s and continues today. To keep the nation's young women fit and healthy, business houses and factories formed marching teams to compete in friendly competition. As the sport took off, the New Zealand Marching Association was founded in 1945, and the heyday of the sport was in the 1950s, when large numbers of teams of midgets, juniors and seniors competed in regional and national competitions, and were judged on their discipline and appearance.

Motor racing

In the 1960s New Zealand produced three of the world's best Formula One grand prix drivers: Chris Amon, Denny Hulme and Bruce McLaren. Amon was third in four European grand prix in 1967, and won the 24-hour Le Mans in France the previous year. Hulme, the son of a Victoria Cross holder, won at Le Mans in 1962, and was Formula One world champion in 1966. He died from a heart attack while racing in Australia. McLaren, with Hulme, won the CanAm Challenge series on five occasions from 1967 to 1971. He died in an accident while testing a car in England in 1970, but his name was maintained by the McLaren racing team and McLaren cars.

Woodchopping

The need to clear bush for farmland led to the sport of woodchopping in New Zealand. Prizes were awarded for different techniques, including the standing and underhand chop, tree felling and both single- and double-handed sawing. It is believed to have begun in Tasmania in the 1880s, and by the early 1900s such competitions had become a regular part of this country's numerous Agricultural and Pastoral (A&P) shows (see page 225). Woodchopping events usually began with the judge's call: 'Axemen stand by your blocks!'

New Zealanders have also won a number of world titles in the sport and in 1960 two New Plymouth axemen chopped through a 14 inch (350 mm) block in 14.8 seconds, easily beating a power-saw operator!

Speedway

Speedway came to New Zealand in 1928 when motorcycle races were held at English Park, Christchurch. Races were held at Kilbirnie, Wellington, the following year, and also at Auckland's Western Springs track. A national body was formed in 1949, with authority over tracks and competitors racing midget and three-quarter midget cars, sidecars, stockcars, modified saloon cars and motorcycles. There are now 23 speedway tracks around the country.

New Zealand speedway has also produced a world champion, Christchurch-born Ivan Mauger. He went to England in 1963, and by 1979 he had won 15 world titles, and among other achievements had captained the British world cup team.

The chips are flying during the woodchopping event at the Malvern Show, Canterbury, in March 2009.

Crouch, touch, ENGAGE 103

Sport

The word sport is used in New Zealand, as in Australia, to describe someone's camaraderie or team spirit. Thus, someone who 'plays the game' is called a good sport. Conversely, someone who doesn't play fair is called a bad sport. In earlier times the term was a common form of address, for males, as in 'G'day, sport'.

Paddock

The word paddock, which in New Zealand usually means a fenced area of farmland (see page 217), is also used to refer to a sports field. For example, a rugby player can be described as 'having a good day on the paddock'.

Offsider

In New Zealand the word offside is most likely to be heard on the sports field, especially rugby. An offsider, however, usually has nothing to do with sport. An offsider is an assistant to another more experienced worker. The term usually relates to apprentice tradesmen, such as carpenters and electricians.

Zam-buk and the Order of St John

Zam-buk is an all-purpose ointment containing, among other things, eucalyptus and camphor. Originally from England, it was also made in Australia and could be bought in New Zealand from the early 1900s. It is still available today. Before long, the name Zam-buk was being applied to the uniformed members of the Order of St John who carried out volunteer first aid at sports meetings, where they made liberal use of the ointment. The St John's organisation began in this country in 1885, and was soon established in small towns where there were few medical services but frequent injuries in the workforce.

Fair dinkum FUN

Country halls

The country hall was a feature of New Zealand's rural landscape in the first half of the twentieth century. Usually a simple building — with weatherboard cladding and a corrugated iron roof — it was at the heart of every local community and the venue for dances, social occasions and community events. Halls were built in memory of local pioneers, or as war memorials in honour of locals who had died on service overseas. For dances the halls were decorated with floral arrangements, and the floor was sprinkled with powder in preparation for set dances, including foxtrots, quicksteps, and Gay Gordons. A lavish supper, made by the locals, was laid out on trestle tables. Times changed in the period following the Second World War, and the country hall was no longer such an important focus for the community.

Weekly News

The *Weekly News*, with its distinctive pink cover — also known as the *Auckland Weekly* — first appeared on 28 November 1863. It was the longest surviving and best known of the news magazines launched in New Zealand in the nineteenth century. Published in Auckland by Wilson & Horton, who also produced the daily *New Zealand Herald* newspaper, the *Weekly News* described itself as: 'A journal of commerce, agriculture, politics, literature, science, and art'. It was an immediate success and became well known for its centre section of high-quality photographs of world and local news events. However, with competition from new forms of media, sales declined and the last edition appeared on 23 August 1971.

New Zealand Woman's Weekly

The *New Zealand Woman's Weekly* was launched in December 1932. It is one of the great survivors in the highly competitive world of women's magazines — celebrating its seventy fifth birthday in 2007. The *Weekly* has become part of New Zealand home life, providing a weekly selection of handy hints, recipes, fashion and glamour, news and gossip from New Zealand and overseas. The lives of celebrities, and the British royal family in particular, have always played an important part in the *Woman's Weekly*. For example, the issue featuring the wedding of Prince Charles and Princess Diana in 1981 was one of the magazine's biggest sellers, and Diana is still the all-time most-popular cover star.

The magazine has moved with the times to reflect the changing interests and lifestyles of New Zealand women, and more than 950,000 New Zealanders read the *Woman's Weekly* every week.

Yarning

While Maori have a long tradition of oral story-telling, the word yarning came to New Zealand from Australia in the mid-1800s. It means passing the time by telling stories, much like 'spinning yarn'. A yarn is not necessarily a tall, or untrue, tale, but many certainly are.

In the 1960s Barry Crump became known for his stories written in a style described as a literary yarn — they were simple and humorous, reflecting the everyday manner of the ordinary Kiwi bloke who wanted to go bush by living an independent and less complicated life away from the city.

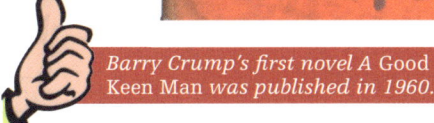

Barry Crump's first novel A Good Keen Man *was published in 1960.*

Fair dinkum FUN 109

Country Women's Institute

In 1921 the New Zealand Federation of Country Women's Institutes (CWI) was established, at Rissington, Hawke's Bay, with a view to assisting rural women by providing education and training in a range of agricultural and domestic subjects. An Auckland federation began in 1927, followed by Wellington a year later, and by the mid-1960s the national organisation had 1015 individual institutes and a total of 36,354 members.

There have been several name changes over the years and in 2008 it became The New Zealand Federation of Women's Institutes with 445 local institutes and over 8000 members.

Ladies, a plate

From about the 1930s, men might be charged admission to certain social events while women were required to provide a contribution towards the supper. Hence the following words might appear on an invitation to a gathering at the local hall: 'Gents 2/6, Ladies a Plate'.

Peggy squares

Small knitted squares, which were sewn together, often as rugs to be sold for fundraising purposes, were known as peggy squares. They were named after a young Hutt Valley girl, Peggy Huse. In 1932 Peggy knitted a large number of squares that were made into bedcovers for people in need of warm blankets.

Wearable Arts

••

The World of Wearable Arts — WOW — was created by Suzie Moncrieff of Nelson in 1987, and began as a promotion for a rural art gallery. It grew into an annual extravaganza of art and fashion and in 2005 the show moved to Wellington. The awards attract entries from New Zealand and around the world, and some 150 garments are shown in a lavish and unforgettable performance that attracts 35,000 every year. From the futuristic to the theatrical, all manner of material is incorporated into fashion and is set to a music, lighting and special-effects show like nothing you've ever seen before.

Centennial Exhibition

••

The Centennial Exhibition in Wellington, on show from November 1939 until April 1940, was the main event to mark 100 years of British sovereignty over New Zealand. The exhibition received 2,641,043 visitors. Playland, an amusement park associated with the exhibition, proved even more popular, attracting 2,870,995 visitors.

Pasifika

••

Maori culture evolved from this country's first Polynesian settlers. New immigrants from the Pacific began arriving in increasing numbers from the 1950s, seeking work opportunities. Most of them settled in Auckland. Since 1993 Auckland has recognised its strong South Pacific connections with the annual Pasifika Festival held throughout the region to celebrate art, culture and lifestyles from around the Pacific. The first event attracted 30,000 visitors, and it grew rapidly from there. The festival now enjoys over 225,000 visitors and all the Pacific nations are represented, offering displays of music, dancing and traditional arts and food.

The flicks

Because of their flickery nature, a trip to the movies was referred to as 'going to the flicks'. The first commercial screenings of a silent film were in the United States in 1896 and within a few years films were showing in this country. New Zealand's towns and cities soon had picture houses with such names as Roxy, Royal, Princess, Britannia, His Majesty's and The Grand. By 1950 we had 600 cinemas, and at the end of that decade there was one cinema seat for every 7.5 citizens — that was a world record we shared with Australia.

It's in the Bag

The game show *It's in the Bag*, hosted by Selwyn Toogood (see page 131), was one of New Zealand's most popular radio programmes in the 1950s and 1960s. The show required contestants who answered questions correctly to choose between the money and the bag. The prizes in the bags included the latest in whiteware, clothing and homeware, but there were also some booby prizes to add to the excitement. Several of Selwyn Toogood's signature phrases from the show soon became part of Kiwi vernacular, e.g. 'By hokey!' and 'The money or the bag?'. In the 1970s Selwyn Toogood hosted the show on television and after his retirement the show was hosted by John Hawkesby followed by Nick Tansley.

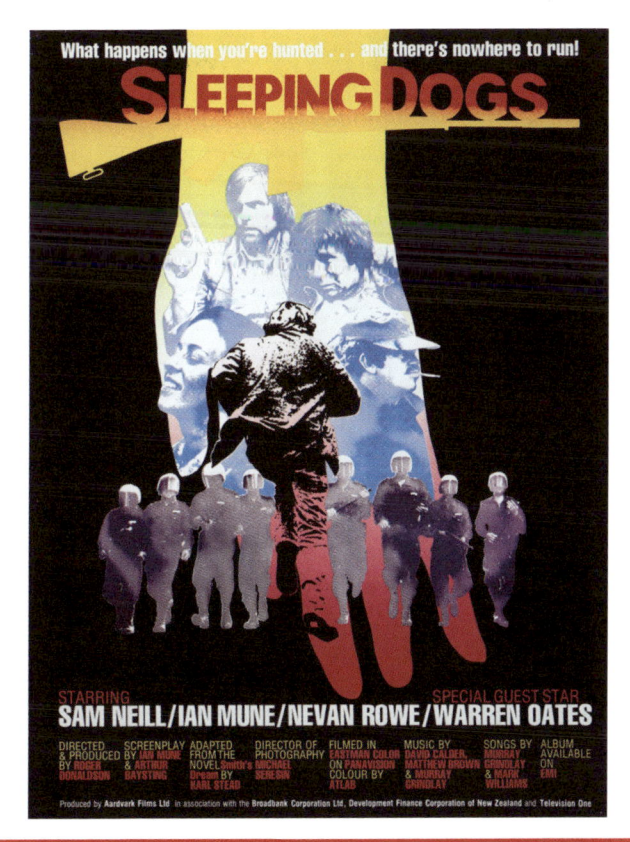

The 1977 New Zealand film Sleeping Dogs, *directed by Roger Donaldson and based on the 1971 novel*, Smith's Dream, *by C.K. Stead.*

Fair dinkum FUN 113

'Pokarekare Ana'

One of the best known songs to have been produced by New Zealand, and sung by New Zealanders overseas, is the love song, 'Pokarekare Ana'. It was written by East Coast Maori songwriter Paraire Tomoana and popularised by Maori soldiers based at an Auckland army camp during the First World War. It was first published in 1921.

'Blue Smoke'

In 1940, following the outbreak of war, Dannevirke farmhand and musician Ruru Karaitiana joined the Maori Battalion and went overseas on the troopship *Aquitania*. While the ship was off the coast of Africa a friend drew his attention to some passing smoke, which inspired him to write the song 'Blue Smoke'. He performed the song at concerts for troops during the war, but it was rejected by a music publishing company in London. Back in Wellington after the war, Karaitiana assembled a group of musicians — which included his future wife Pixie Williams — and in 1948 recorded a version of the song for the local record label TANZA (which stands for To Assist New Zealand Artists). It was the first record to be entirely produced in this country, from composition to pressing, and it quickly became a big seller — among others, it was recorded by American crooner Dean Martin.

'She's a Mod'

In 1964 Christchurch-born Ray Columbus and his group, the Invaders, recorded a song which, for many young New Zealanders, caught the spirit of the decade. Written by an English composer, 'She's a Mod' was released while the Beatles were touring this country and capitalised on their popularity with its persistent 'yeah yeah yeah' refrain. It was the first New Zealand record to top the charts in Australia. Shortly after, it topped the charts at home, too.

'Ten Guitars'

In 1967 English singer Engelbert Humperdinck — whose real name was Gerry Dorsey and who took the name of a nineteenth century Austrian composer — recorded the hugely successful 'Please Release Me'. But it was the flip-side of the record, the song 'Ten Guitars', that proved more popular in New Zealand at parties and in the nation's shearing sheds. There have been about a dozen local recorded versions of the song.

'Poi E'

In 1982 linguist Ngoi Pewhairangi and musician Dalvanius Prime wrote 'Poi E' to teach young Maori to be proud of their heritage. Record companies were not interested in the song, so Prime formed his own company, Maui Records, and recorded the song sung by the Patea Maori Club. It was on the New Zealand music charts for 22 weeks in 1984, including four weeks at number one. Later that year the Patea Maori Club toured the United Kingdom, increasing the popularity of the infectious 'Poi E'.

In 2002 Dalvanius Prime was honoured with a special award from Te Waka Toi, the Maori section of Creative New Zealand, for his contribution to Maori arts, and died later that year in Hawera, aged 54.

Radio

New Zealand's first major radio station — 1YA — went to air in Auckland in 1926, followed quickly by 3YA in Christchurch and 2YA in Wellington in mid-1927. In March 1936 the New Zealand Parliament broadcast its proceedings over the radio — it was the first Commonwealth country to do so. Before long this country had eight national broadcasting stations and 22 privately owned stations.

For about 30 years, families would gather around the wireless in the evenings and receive news, entertainment and education. However, the arrival of television in June 1960 meant stiff competition. Eleven years later the radio licence — the fee was 5/- (5 shillings) when it began in 1923 — was abolished and replaced by a television licence fee of $20.

Pirate radio

In 1935 the government closed down or assumed control of all independent radio stations. To break the state monopoly, and in response to the state-owned broadcasting services' inability to reflect social taste and play popular music, in November 1966 the country's first 'pirate' radio station, Hauraki, put to sea from Auckland in the ship *Tiri*. Radio Hauraki began transmitting from international waters, beyond the then three-mile — now 22-kilometre — limit.

Howard Morrison

In 1956 Rotorua-born Maori entertainer Howard Morrison formed a group with his brother Laurie, cousin John and a friend,

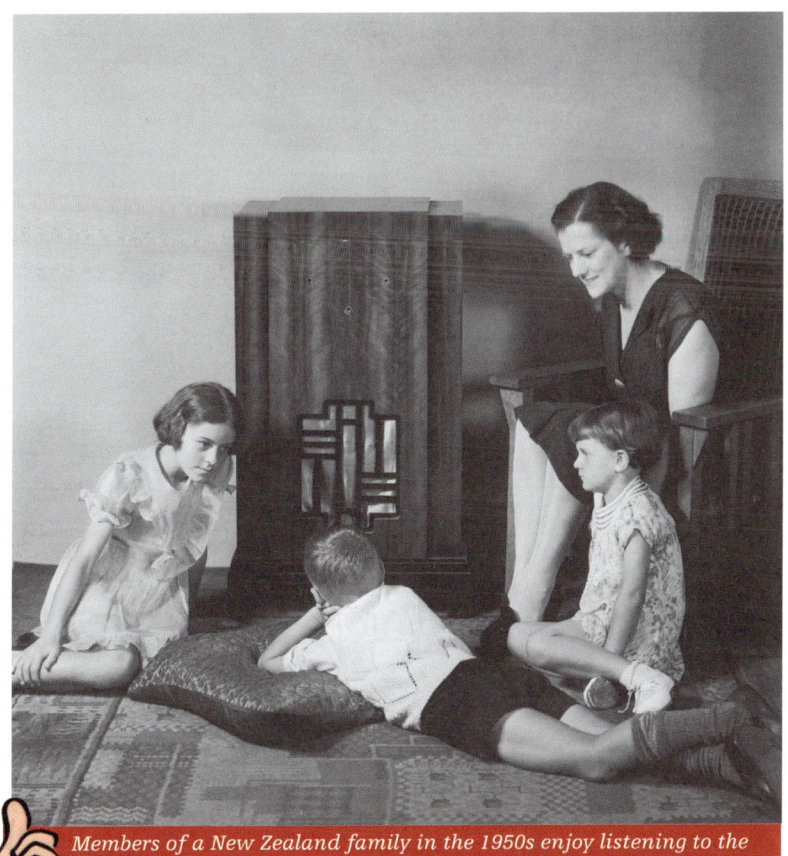

Members of a New Zealand family in the 1950s enjoy listening to the radio, or wireless. In the days before television, the valve radio cabinet was a major item of furniture in the nation's lounges.

Fair dinkum FUN 117

guitarist Gerry Merito. It became the Howard Morrison Quartet and they released their first record in 1958. In 1959 the group completed a nationwide tour and recorded the first of a number of extremely popular parodies — 'The Battle of Waikato' was based on 'The Battle of New Orleans' as sung by Johnny Horton and Lonnie Donegan. In 1960 Wi Wharekura and Noel Kingi joined the group. More popular parodies followed, including 'Mori the Hori', based on Ray Stevens' 'Ahab the Arab', which was highly topical that year as Maori players were not allowed to tour South Africa with the All Blacks. The group disbanded in 1964 and Howard Morrison began his solo career, leading to his performance at the opening ceremony of the Commonwealth Games and his knighthood in 1990.

Split Enz

The first New Zealand rock group to break into the British and United States markets began performing in Auckland in 1971, when they were known as Split Ends. Four years later they moved to Australia and changed their name to Split Enz, acknowledging their country of origin. The group then went to England, where their single 'I See Red' gained attention. Back in New Zealand in 1980, they recorded the internationally successful album *True Colours*. The single 'I Got You' topped charts in Australia, Canada and New Zealand, and was followed by the success of the albums *Waiata* (1981) and *Time and Tide* (1982). The latter album included the single 'Six Months in a Leaky Boat', which was caught up in controversy when released in Britain. Although recorded before the Falklands War began, it was removed from radio playlists because references to leaking boats were a sensitive issue at a time of British naval casualties.

In 1984 Split Enz disbanded and their lead singer, the Te Awamutu-born Tim Finn, established a solo career. His brother Neil enjoyed international success with his group Crowded House (which Tim later joined).

Television

Some closed circuit broadcasts were made in the early 1950s and regular transmission of television in New Zealand began in Auckland in 1960. Wellington and Christchurch had to wait until 1961, and Dunedin until 1962. A second network, known as TV2, began transmitting from Auckland and Christchurch in 1975, and a third channel, TV3, was launched in late 1989. New Zealand televiewers now have an increasing range of channels to choose from, including C4, Prime Maori TV, Sky and Freeview.

From 1960 until it was abolished in 1999, New Zealanders were required to pay a television licence fee, later known as the public broadcasting fee. These funds, used for the production of programmes, were administered by New Zealand On Air, which is now supported directly by a Government grant.

Telethon

The first telethon — a televised 24-hour fundraising event with performances by a wide range of local and international entertainers — was held by TV2 in 1975 during the station's opening week. Volunteers collected money and telephone operators took promises of donations, while a running tally of the amount raised was displayed in the studio and on screen. The first telethon raised nearly $600,000 for the St John Ambulance service. The 1981 telethon raised $5 million for the

International Year of Disabled Persons, and the events continued until 1990, only to be resurrected once more in 2009. New Zealanders of all ages have always 'got in behind' a good cause. Many a 30- or 40-something Kiwi can remember the special childhood treat of camping out in the lounge in sleeping bags, trying desperately to stay awake all night so as to not miss a moment of Telethon.

The Goodnight Kiwi

From 1980 until 1994 the last thing seen each night on TV1 and TV2 was the Goodnight Kiwi. This one-minute-long animation showed the kiwi — with his cat — closing down transmission, turning out the light and putting out the milk bottle before climbing the transmission mast to sleep in a satellite dish.

On 1 December 2008 Television New Zealand brought back an animated sequence of a new-look Goodnight Kiwi — and his cat — for the Christmas and summer holiday period.

Country Calendar

In March 1966 New Zealanders were introduced to a television programme that became, in the words of TVNZ, the country's longest-running series 'by a country mile'. *Country Calendar* began as a television version of the daily farming radio programme. It quickly proved popular, winning awards at the Feltex Television Awards in 1975, 1977, 1980, 1981, 1982 and 1983. To celebrate its fortieth birthday in 2006, an hour-long special-feature presented highlights from some of the programme's earliest days, including famous spoofs on radio-controlled sheep dogs and musical farmers plucking number-eight fencing wire. Now into its fourty-second season, the show has continuing popularity suggesting that, while most New Zealanders live in towns and cities, they still have a strong interest in the rural sector.

Fair Go

'Fair go!' was an international expression used in New Zealand from the late 1920s that meant, 'Come on, be reasonable'. The phrase took on a new lease of life when it became the name of a locally produced consumer-affairs television programme in 1977. *Fair Go* proved popular, and was a winner at the Feltex Television Awards in 1978 and 1979. Thirty-one years later it is still going strong, and in 2006 it was the sixth most-watched series on New Zealand television.

Shortland Street

Shortland Street is New Zealand's longest-running locally made television soap opera. It first screened on 25 May 1992. Although there is a Shortland Street in Auckland, the programme is set in and around a fictional Auckland-based hospital of the same name. By 1999, when the show was attracting some 600,000 viewers each night, sociologists claimed it was no longer just a soap opera but had become a cultural institution. The show has produced many actors who have gone on to pursue successful local and international stage and screen careers, including internationally acclaimed actors Martin Henderson and Temuera Morrison. The most famous line ever from the show is undoubtedly: 'You're not in Guatemala now, Dr Ropata.'

Fair dinkum FUN

Outrageous Fortune

In 2005 New Zealand was introduced to the comedy-drama television series *Outrageous Fortune*. It related the (mis)adventures of the Wests, described as a 'one-family crime wave'. When it completed its fourth season in 2008 it qualified as the longest-running drama made in New Zealand (although *Shortland Street* has been running much longer, because it has half-hour episodes it is considered a soap opera). The fifth series of *Outrageous Fortune* began in June 2009.

Footrot Flats

Murray Ball's comic strip *Footrot Flats* first appeared in the *Evening Post* newspaper in 1976. Set on a New Zealand farm, it told of the adventures of Wallace (known as Wal) Footrot, his sheepdog (known as Dog) and other animals on his farm called Footrot Flats. Ball was born in Fielding in 1937, and worked in England where he achieved success with his strip *Stanley*. He returned to New Zealand and was living on a farm near Gisborne when he began writing *Footrot Flats*. After succeeding in New Zealand, the strip appeared in newspapers in Australia and Europe. In 1986 it also inspired an award-winning film, *Footrot Flats: the Dog's ~~Tail~~ Tale*. The theme song 'A Slice of Heaven' by Dave Dobbyn was a chart-topper in New Zealand and Australia.

Lord of the Rings

The Lord of the Rings is a movie trilogy produced by Peter Jackson. It is based on J.R.R. Tolkien's trilogy of books by the same name. The three films — *The Fellowship of the Ring* (2001), *The Two Towers* (2002) and *The Return of the King* (2003) — were set in the fictional world of Middle Earth and filmed in locations around New Zealand. The trilogy was a huge financial success, and won a staggering 17 Academy Awards.

Weta Workshop

In recent years New Zealand's nastiest-looking insect (see page 270) has received positive promotion in the name of Weta Workshop, the award winning special effects company that has worked on such movies as Peter Jackson's *The Lord of the Rings* and *King Kong*.

Buzzy Bee

Perhaps the best-known example of Kiwiana is a small wooden pull-along toy bee, painted in red, yellow, blue and black with whirring wings and quivering antennae. It started life in the woodworking factory of Auckland brothers Hec and John Ramsey, who began making children's toys in 1941. Buzzy Bee went into production seven years later, part of a range of toys that included Richard Rabbit, Oscar Ostrich, Percy Penguin, Dorable Duck, Kriss Kricket, Peter Pup, Katie Caterpillar and Alli-Gator.

While the bee is considered distinctly New Zealand, it seems the idea actually came from the United States — from a toy with the same name made by Fisher-Price in New York. Their bee had the familiar sound effects, wobbly antennae and revolving wings. The big difference was in the body shape — theirs was made of a flat piece of wood covered with printed paper. New Zealand's Buzzy Bee was much more bee-like, being fully rounded, and initially it was turned out of native tawa timber. The Buzzy Bee got some great publicity in 1983 when local media showed a baby by the name of Prince William playing with the toy, on a royal visit to New Zealand with his parents Prince Charles and Princess Diana.

Fun Ho!

For nearly 50 years New Zealand children enjoyed this locally produced range of colourful toys. In 1935 Jack Underwood began making small lead figures, including footballers and soldiers, in his Wellington basement. He later set up a factory in Inglewood, Taranaki, and from 1942 produced sand-cast aluminium toys, including a large range of vehicles, such as tractors, trucks, planes and trains. These toys were strong and durable, and often put to hard work in the nation's sandpits. Growing competition from imported plastic toys forced the factory to close in 1987, but three years later the Fun Ho! National Toy Museum opened. Replicas of original Fun Ho! toys are still made, and owners can buy spare parts from the museum in Inglewood.

Scouts

In 1908 Lieutenant-General Baden-Powell launched the scouting movement in Britain, and it reached New Zealand the same year. Eight years later, cub scouts were introduced and younger members could join. Scouts provided an early opportunity for New Zealand boys to learn practical outdoor skills, including how to tie knots and how to build a campfire. In 1987 girls were admitted to scouts. In 2007, following a rapid decline in membership, the national body introduced 'new scouting' to increase numbers. The following year, 2008, marked the centenary of scouting in New Zealand.

Girl Guides

The girl guide movement began in New Zealand in 1908, shortly after the founding of the scouting movement. The first guide patrols were formed in 1922, and the movement's membership grew steadily until the mid-1980s when it began to decline. Girls were required to learn skills with a view to earning 'badges' in such areas as cooking, sewing, first aid and various outdoor pursuits.

Cereal cards

Since the 1930s New Zealanders have at various times received free collectable cards in their cereal packets. The Timaru Milling Company began its first series of cards in packets of O-TIS and Oatlets in 1936 — the original cards were on the theme of flight and aircraft, and Peter the Pilot was a favourite from 1939 to 1954. The largest source of cards has been Weet-Bix whose 'Treasury of the Years' series ran from 1941 until 1955. New sets of Weet-Bix cards then appeared at least once a year, and included 'Evolution of Flight' (1956), 'National Costumes and Flags' (1959), 'Cavalcade of Cars' (1962), 'What Makes New Zealand Different' (1967), 'Our South Pacific Neighbours' (1974) and '1990: Look How We've Grown' (1990).

One of the best collections of Weet-Bix cards is that of a Waikato farmer from Walton, Derek Lugton. He began collecting at the age of eight and has a complete set of more than 3000 cards. Among his collection is the most sought-after series 'Advance Anzac', from 1946, including the rarest of all Weet-Bix cards, that of Air Force Squadron Leader Leonard Trent, who was awarded the Victoria Cross.

Cereal toys

Free toys in New Zealand cereal boxes first appeared in 1956 with the Timaru Milling Company's set of 30 small plastic Olympic athletes in 1956 — the year the Olympic Games were held in Melbourne, Australia. The following year Sanitarium put out the first of its many sets, beginning with aircraft and racing cars. One of the more unusual items was a small plastic submarine produced in 1958 — with the addition of a small quantity of baking soda, this vessel could operate in a bath of water. Sanitarium continued to provide toys in its products until 2000.

Junior Digest

In 1945 New Zealand boys and girls had their own locally produced — in Christchurch — monthly magazine, *Junior Digest*. Pocket-sized, like the adults' *Reader's Digest*, it provided wholesome reading and claimed to be 'packed with pleasure'. It survived for 20 years, until December 1965.

Smoking

Smoking was introduced to New Zealand Maori by the first European visitors, who traded tobacco for clay pipes. This country proved suitable for growing tobacco and one of the more successful companies in the 1930s, the Napier-based National Tobacco Company, produced Riverhead Gold and Desert Gold, which became household names. Whether the preference was for 'roll your owns' or ready-made cigarettes, by the 1950s a large proportion of adult New Zealanders were smoking and tobacco companies stressed the reputedly 'healthy'

Kauri tobacco was a product of the St James Tobacco Company of New Zealand, which operated in Motueka from the late 1940s

Fair dinkum FUN

aspects of their products in their advertising. Since then New Zealand has led the world in the introduction of anti-smoking legislation, recognising that some 5000 deaths per year are attributable to direct smoking or inhaling second-hand smoke.

Art Union and Golden Kiwi

The 1929 visit to New Zealand by Charles Kingsford Smith increased public interest in aviation, and led to a number of government-approved art unions, or lotteries, to raise money for developing aerodromes. Other organisations soon implemented their own fundraisers, and in 1932 the government took control, authorising the government-controlled Art Union as the only legal form of lottery.

In 1961 the Golden Kiwi lottery replaced the old Art Union, with a £30,000 first prize and another 1800 prizes worth a total of £30,000. The 5/- (5 shilling) tickets were popular Christmas and birthday presents, and decorated smoko rooms around the country. The Golden Kiwi offered armchair millionaires hope until 1989 when, with the arrival of the Lotteries Commission, it was replaced with the dollar-a-scratch Instant Kiwi. During its career the Golden Kiwi had distributed some $600 million to 3.5 million lucky New Zealanders.

Lotto and Instant Kiwi

The first Lotto draw took place on 1 August 1987. The weekly draw is filmed at Avalon Studios, Lower Hutt, and televised live on Saturday nights. To date more than $3.75 billion has been paid out in prizes to more than 63.4 million lucky Lotto players.

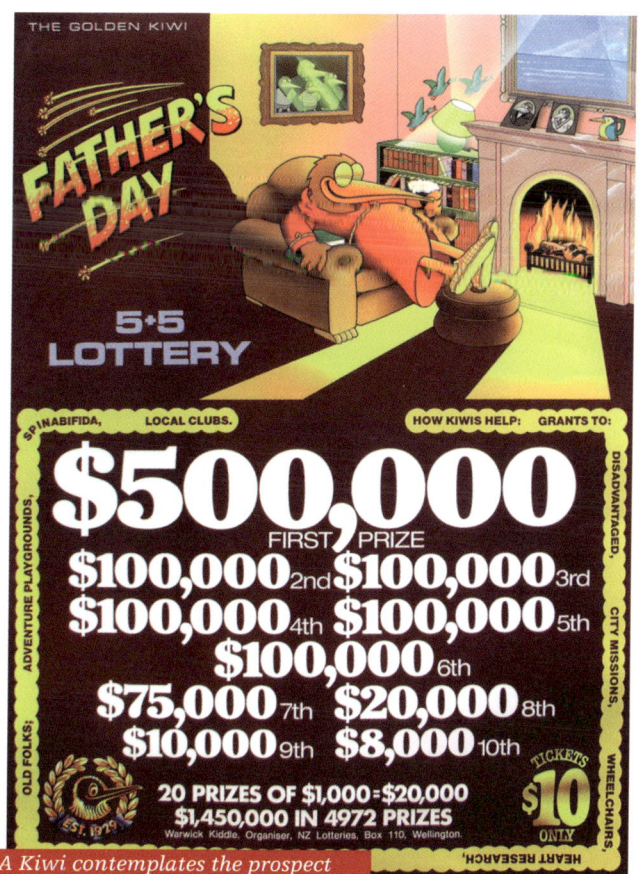

A Kiwi contemplates the prospect of spending half a million dollars.

Cards for the Instant Kiwi scratch-card lottery, introduced in 1989, are sold at Lotto retailers, and at any one time there are at least 12 different games to choose from. The tickets cost between $1 and $10, and offer players the chance to win prizes ranging from $2 to $250,000.

Bottle drives

Drinks, including alcohol and soft drinks, used to come in bottles that had a refundable deposit built into the purchase price. At the time, collecting bottles in 'bottle drives' was a popular means of raising money for community groups, such as schools, scout troops and sports clubs. In the 1960s, the refund on standard soft drink bottles was 3d (threepence).

Bullrush

This rough-and-tumble children's game requires a large number of energetic participants. To begin, one player stands in the middle of a large, open ground and attempts to tag or tackle the other players who rush en masse from one side of the field to the other. Tagged players stay in the middle and the survivors have to run back in the other direction without being tagged, and so on, until there is just one player left untagged who is declared the winner. Today, bullrush is banned in most schools due to its potential for causing serious physical injury.

Brian Sutton-Smith, born in New Zealand in 1924, who trained as a teacher and studied children's games, recorded over 50 early names for variations of Bullrush. The most common of these was Bar the Door, while there was also King Caesar and Punch King.

The Tuis

Today, the Recording Industry Association of New Zealand acknowledges the best in various categories of locally produced music with its annual New Zealand Music Awards, otherwide known as 'The Tuis' after the native New Zealand bird with the beautiful song.

A First World War concert party and the New Zealand Women's Auxiliary Army Corps in the Second World War were also both known as the Tuis.

Selwyn Toogood

Selwyn Toogood, born in Wellington in 1916, became New Zealand's best-known quiz-master. Returning home on a troopship after the Second World War, he ran his first quiz show, and back in Wellington began his career as an actor and radio announcer. Toogood became a household name with *It's in the Bag* (see page 112). From 1976 to 1985 he presented the daily agony-aunt-style television show called *Beauty and the Beast* with a panel of women, and in 1979 he published his autobiography *Out of the Bag*. He died in 2001.

Peter Cape

Peter Cape, born in Helensville in 1926, wrote songs about rural New Zealand. Some are considered classics of their type, in particular: 'Down the Hall on Saturday Night' and 'Taumarunui on the Main Trunk Line: A New Zealand Joker's Lament for his Sheila'. The son of a door-to-door salesman, Cape was educated by Correspondence School. After obtaining a BA at Auckland University he worked as a journalist, and for the New Zealand Broadcasting Service. He recorded his first songs in the late 1950s, and later wrote about the arts and crafts of New Zealand. He died in 1979.

Kiri Te Kanawa

Operatic soprano Kiri Te Kanawa was born in Gisborne in 1944, and educated at St Mary's College in Auckland. She studied singing under Sister Mary Leo from 1959 to 1965, the year she won both the New Zealand Mobil Song Quest and the Melbourne Sun Aria competition. The following year she moved to London, to study and sing, and soon established herself as an international opera star. New Zealand's best known living singer, she became Dame Kiri Te Kanawa in 1982.

Fred Dagg

The fictional and comic figure of Fred Dagg was created and performed by John Clarke on New Zealand television from 1973 to 1976. Dagg was a stereotypical New Zealand farmer, wearing a crumpled hat, torn shorts, black singlet and gumboots, and frequently seen with a number of similar rural types, all named Trev. He also had an extremely successful singing career, which included 'We Don't Know How Lucky We Are' and 'The Gumboot Song'. Dagg also starred in the 1977 movie *Dagg Day Afternoon*. In 1979, Clarke moved to Australia, where he established himself as a top political satirist, and in 2002 he donated Fred Dagg's gumboots to the collection of Te Papa Tongarewa.

Crikey!

Lynn of Tawa

Lynn of Tawa — named after an outer suburb of Wellington — was created and performed by comedian Ginette McDonald and began appearing on New Zealand's television screens in the late 1970s. She satirised the nation's suburban lifestyle and speech habits, in particular the use of grating vowels and a rising intonation on the last few words in a statement so that every sentence sounds like a question. In 1981, while performing at The Royal Variety Concert before the Queen and Prince Philip, Lynn offered the nation's blessing to Her Majesty: 'God Bless You. We all love you, eh'.

Topp Twins

Jools and Lynda Topp, born in Huntly in 1958, are New Zealand's top folk singing comedy duo, and have been performing for more than 25 years. Their cast of characters includes Camp Mother (in her pink velour jumpsuit) and Camp Leader; typical Kiwi bloke Ken (Moller) from Wairarapa and his best mate Ken (Smythe), a townie; the Gingham Sisters (Belle and Belle), who specialise in country music and yodelling, and Prue and Dolly, two socialites from an old-money Hawkes Bay family. The Topp Twins were inducted into the New Zealand Music Hall of Fame in 2008, and the following year were the subject of the documentary *Untouchable Girls*.

Up the BOOHAI

Boohai

There are various spellings including boo-ai, boo-ay and boo-hai for this word used to describe a remote place or district. It is usually used in the expression 'up the boohai'. It comes from Puhoi, a once remote township north of Auckland that was settled by German-speaking Bohemians from Staab in what is now the Czech Republic.

Baches and cribs

The simple New Zealand holiday house, usually located at the beach or lake, is known as a bach in the North Island and northern part of the South Island. The name bach comes from bachelor, representing the single men who worked on farms in the early days and lived in basic huts on their own — their basic lifestyle was known as baching. Although an early reference to the term crib was in an Auckland newspaper in 1852, which contrasted the 'merchant in his comptoir' [counting house, or office] with the 'huckster [pedlar] in his crib', it is now only used in the southern part of the South Island.

A classic New Zealand bach has only one or two rooms, and is made of simple, often recycled, materials, including fibrolite and corrugated iron. Inside, it has old furniture and fittings retired from the owners' main house back in the suburbs. An outside tank provides water collected off the roof. Somewhere on the section there's an outside dunny and a simple clothesline for togs (see page 65) and towels. The lawn around a basic bach is likely to be kikuyu, and littered with surfboards, canoes and other play equipment. The bach once offered an easier and more casual lifestyle, like camping, but such retreats are now an endangered species, a result of stricter regulations, the increasing cost of land, and the tendency for holiday homes to match suburban homes.

Katherine Mansfield provided a wonderful description of baches based on childhood memories of her family holidays at Day's Bay, Wellington, in her short story, 'At the Bay', written in Switzerland and first published in 1922: 'Over the verandahs, prone on the paddock, flung over the fences . . . were exhausted-looking bathing-dresses and rough-striped towels. Each back window seemed to have a pair of sand-shoes on the sill and some lumps of rock or a bucket or a collection of pawa [paua] shells.'

Trailer sailer

The trailer sailer is a sailing boat, usually under eight metres long and made of plywood, that can easily be constructed by a home builder. A retractable keel means they can be easily transported on a trailer. They were introduced to New Zealand in the mid-1960s and quickly became extremely popular.

Thermette

In 1929 John Ashley Hart, who had an electrical business in Auckland, invented a small portable outdoor water boiler which he named the Thermette. It is a cylindrical device with a riveted handle, and a water-jacket that surrounds an internal fire box. Some crumpled paper, a few small sticks and dry twigs are placed in the fire box and lit with a match, and within minutes the water is boiling and ready for a cuppa.

A basic New Zealand bach, handily located just a few steps from the beach.

Up the BOOHAI 137

Thermettes were produced in a range of colours — blue, orange and green. In the late 1930s, as the Second World War approached, the New Zealand Army got to hear about the handy little boiler and the Thermette became standard equipment for New Zealanders fighting in North Africa, where it was renamed the Benghazi Boiler. The idea of the Thermette soon spread to other countries. They are still available today.

A recent invention from Otago physiotherapist Steve August called the Kiwitub takes the water-heating principle of the Thermette and up-sizes it to heat a portable spa pool. It takes just an hour or two to heat up, and, unlike a spa pool, it doesn't require chemicals to keep the water clean.

Chilly bin

In 1974 the Christchurch company Skellerup Industries applied for a patent for a lightweight portable container for food and drink, insulated to keep the contents cool. They called it the chilly bin and it quickly became popular for picnics and outings at the beach. Before long chilly bin became a generic name, which meant any type of container that kept food cool. The Australian equivalent is the esky, which is another trade name that has become generic — the original name was an abbreviation of Eskimo.

Lilo

From the 1950s the lilo, an inflatable air mattress designed as a portable bed for campers, was essential for a day at the beach. The lilo originally came from England and was made of fabric-covered rubber. Lilos could be large — up to 76 inches (193 cm) long by 30 inches (76 cm) wide. So, they took a while to inflate. Although fun for floating on the surf, lilos were a curse for surf lifesavers as they were at the mercy of wind and currents and could carry unwary occupants out to sea. Beach-goers without a lilo often made do with an inflated tractor inner tube.

Tramping

By the late nineteenth century, deer hunters and mountaineers were attracted to New Zealand's bush and hills. Soon tramping — known as hiking, trekking and rambling in other countries — became a popular recreational activity. It became more organised in 1919 with the establishment of the first tramping club, in Wellington. Others followed around the country, resulting in the building of huts and the cutting of tracks. The tramping clubs of New Zealand enjoyed their greatest membership period from the 1940s through to the 1970s.

Today the Department of Conservation maintains hundreds of walking tracks around the country (there are about 100 in Northland alone), providing for New Zealanders and overseas visitors.

Milford Track

The 55-kilometre-long Milford Track, from the head of Lake Te Anau to the head of Milford Sound, offers a four-day hike through untouched mountain scenery of glaciers, waterfalls and forests. It is New Zealand's most famous hiking track and it follows a route discovered in 1888. In 1908 the Milford Track was described in a London magazine as 'The Finest Walk in the World'.

The Milford Track is one of the Department of Conservation's premier tracks, known as the Great Walks. This category also includes the Tongariro Northern Circuit, Abel Tasman Coast Track, Heaphy Track (in the Kahurangi National Park), Lake Waikaremoana, Routeburn Track (through Mount Aspiring and Fordland National Parks), and Rakiura Track (Stewart Island/Rakiura).

Camping grounds

Tents were originally only used by explorers, then by adventurous types in search of the healthy life outdoors. Recreational camping grounds were established in New Zealand from the mid-1920s with the arrival of private cars. They provided basic cooking and bathroom facilities, but a pioneering spirit was still needed when living under canvas.

Recently New Zealand's camping grounds have been under pressure as the value of prime coastal land has risen steeply, and many camping grounds have been sold to property developers. Like the humble bach, the cheap camping holiday at the beach enjoyed by generations of New Zealanders may soon become a thing of the past.

Changing sheds

At New Zealand beaches and swimming pools, swimmers have long been able to change into their togs (see page 65) in these modest structures, usually made of concrete blocks or corrugated iron. Changing sheds at beaches usually provide showers — often just cold-water showers — for washing off sand and salt.

A bunch of blokes and sheilas taking a break from the demands of a camping holiday in the 1970s.

Up the BOOHAI 141

Tiki tours

In the 1940s the Government Tourist Bureau began a new tourist venture it named Tiki Tours. Transport was provided by New Zealand Railways Road Services' buses. The term 'tiki tour' later came to mean a roundabout or scenic way of getting somewhere.

OE

Since at least the early 1900s New Zealanders have travelled 'Home' or to the 'Old Country' in order to retrace their roots and broaden their view of the world. By the 1950s this common practice among young New Zealanders was becoming known as 'overseas experience' or, simply, OE. Young Kiwi travellers are said to be 'going on their OE' or 'getting their big OE', and these days that can mean a backpacking holiday anywhere in the world.

Queen's Birthday

New Zealanders celebrate Queen Elizabeth II's birthday with a public holiday on the Monday following the first weekend in June. However, this is not really Her Majesty's birthday, which actually falls some six weeks earlier.

Bungy jumping

New Zealander A.J. Hackett is generally credited with popularising the idea of people leaping from great heights with lengths of rubber attached to their legs. This idea came from Melanesia, where Pentecost Islanders jump from wooden towers and are pulled up short of the ground by flexible liana vines tied around their ankles. Members of the Oxford University Dangerous Sports Club in England saw a film of the Pentecost Islanders in action and in 1979 made their first jump, off the 76-metre Clifton Suspension Bridge, near Bristol in England. A.J. Hackett was introduced to the dare-devil activity and in 1986 he and a friend jumped off the Greenhithe Bridge, near Auckland. The following year he drew international attention to the possibilities of bungy jumping when he jumped from the Eiffel Tower, in Paris. His international adventure company began in Queenstown, with a 43-metre jump from the Kawarau Bridge.

In recent years New Zealand's geography and climate have encouraged an increasing range of outdoor and 'extreme sports' pursuits, popular with both locals and tourists. Offering varying degrees of danger and physical challenges, they include jet boating, cycling and kayaking.

Man alone

There is a myth of the New Zealand male as a man alone — a strong, silent type who prefers the independent outdoor life to an office environment or the company of others. The term comes from the title of a novel by John Mulgan, first published in 1939. *Man Alone*, the story of a loner, has gone on to become a New Zealand classic.

Tangata WHENUA

The great fleet

In the late nineteenth century scientists promoted the idea of the great fleet, which brought Maori to New Zealand from their Pacific homeland of Hawaiki in 1350. A popular image of this — and probably the most famous history painting ever produced in this country — was produced by Charles F Goldie and Louis John Steele in 1898 and titled *The Arrival of the Maoris in New Zealand*. The story of the fleet was taught in schools, but in recent years it has been discredited. It is now believed that Maori began arriving in New Zealand from the eastern Pacific about 800 years ago, and that some of the early migration traditions may relate to movements within New Zealand.

Hawaiki

According to oral traditions, Hawaiki is the original homeland of Maori and other Polynesian people. The first European record of this idea was made by Joseph Banks, in February 1770, when the *Endeavour* was in the region of Cook Strait. He recorded the name as 'Heawye', and specified that it 'lay to the Northward where [there] were many lands'.

Waka

The Maori word 'waka' is most commonly used to mean a canoe. In 1770, while visiting New Zealand on the *Endeavour*, Sydney Parkinson recorded the Maori word 'hewaca' for canoe. The Maori had ocean-going canoes with outriggers, but the most impressive were the war canoes — waka taua — that had carved prow and stern pieces.

Tangata whenua

Translated as people of the land or soil, tangata whenua can refer to the original people of the land, for example the Maori in Aotearoa/New Zealand, or to the people associated with a particular place or region. In addition to tangata whenua, the term tangata tiriti — people of the treaty — refers to those who came to this country under the authority of the Treaty of Waitangi.

In May 1860 a large assembly of Maori took place at Ngaruawahia, in the Waikato, at which the tangata whenua were described as 'the tribes who called the meeting and provided the food', while the visitors were termed 'hui'.

— *Daily Southern Cross*, 5 June 1860

Turangawaewae

Turangawaewae — meaning 'a place to stand' — is the name of the marae and headquarters of Te Kingitanga, the Maori King Movement, at Ngaruawahia in the Waikato region. For individuals, turangawaewae refers to a piece of land that represents a person's history or identity.

Iwi and hapu

An iwi is a tribe of people who are related by blood. Each iwi might be divided into smaller communities called hapu. On 6 February 1840 Lieutenant Governor Hobson said to each rangatira (chief) who signed the Treaty of Waitangi: '*He iwi tahi tatou*'. He understood it to mean,

A Maori maiden holding a poi and wearing a greenstone tiki and a huia feather in her hair, attracts overseas visitors on this Department of Tourism and Publicity poster from the 1960s.

Tangata WHENUA

'We are now one people', but it seems a more correct translation would have been 'We two peoples together make a nation'.

Tupuna

A tupuna is an ancestor, or grandparent. In 1844 explorer Ernst Dieffenbach visited a Maori village in Rotorua and described how the carved figures provided a family record for Maori. He wrote: 'Each of the representatives of the human figure bears the name of some tupuna, or ancestor, and the whole is actually a carved history.'

— *Daily Southern Cross*, 6 April 1844

Mana

Mana has no exact equivalent in the English language. There are three kinds of mana: mana someone is born with that comes from their whakapapa (genealogy); mana they are given as a result of their actions; and mana that belongs to a group, such as the mana of a marae. However, in recent times it has come to mean the authority, power and influence someone has, as a result of the respect which others give them.

Mana is also the name of 'The Maori news magazine for all New Zealanders', published since 1993.

Utu

The concept of utu is a form of revenge in response to an earlier offence, which may take the form of monetary compensation. For example, in 1842 it was reported that Maori chiefs from Wanganui were prepared to allow Europeans to settle on their land following the payment of some utu. And in 1883 when a Maori whare (and over £300 in banknotes) was destroyed in a fire near Hawera, south Taranaki, it was claimed it was 'burned for utu'.

Utu was also the title of the 1983 New Zealand feature film, directed by Geoff Murphy, which told the story of a Maori warrior's search for vengeance in the 1870s.

Moko

Traditional moko or tattooing was practised according to strict ritual — the intricate designs indicated family connections. It was observed by men on Cook's *Endeavour* in 1769, while sailing north near Bream Bay, and described by Sir Joseph Banks: '[local Maori had] a much larger quantity of *Amoco* or black stains upon their bodys and faces; almost universaly they had a broad spiral on each buttock and many had their thighs almost intirely black, small lines only being left untouchd so that they lookd like stripd breeches'.

Haka

When Captain James Cook visited Poverty Bay in October 1769 he observed a war dance by local Maori. A member of his crew described it in the first written European description of the Maori haka: 'About an hundred of the natives all Arm'd came down on the opposite side of the salt River, drew themselves up in lines. Then with a Regular Jump from Left to Right and the Reverse, They brandish'd Their Weapons, distort'd their mouths, Lolling out their Tongues and Turn'd up the Whites of their Eyes Accompanied with a strong hoarse song . . .'

As well as showing warlike intentions, the haka could also be performed as a welcome or a challenge on the sports' field. Today the best-known Maori haka is probably 'Ka Mate, Ka Mate', composed around 1820 by warrior Te Rauparaha. He wrote it at a time when he was taking part in a battle with another chief, and sought the safety of a kumara pit. He recited this haka as he returned to battle.

In 1857 'Ka Mate' was performed by Maori at an Auckland function attended by the Governor. At the time it was described as 'the peace-making song' and today it is performed before test matches by the All Blacks.

This was how it was translated in 1857:

Ka mate, ka mate!	It is dead, is dead!
Ka ora, ka ora!	It lives, it lives!
Tenei te tangata puhuruhuru	Here is the man with the hairy limbs
Nana I tiki mai	who came forward
I whakawhiti te ra!	and caused the sun to shine forth.
Upane! Upane!	It strikes, it smites.
Whiti te ra!	Bright shines the sun.

— *Daily Southern Cross*, 13 November 1857

Powhiri

A powhiri is a welcoming ceremony, which can take place on a marae or anywhere that the tangata whenua want to formally greet visitors. Traditionally a powhiri would follow 10 basic steps, but it can be adapted according to the occasion.

A powhiri welcoming people on to Te Kaha Marae to celebrate the awarding of the Victoria Cross to Corporal Willie Apiata, 12 August 2007.

Hui

A hui is a special gathering, usually of a large number of people and taking place over several days. Such occasions are at the heart of Maori life and have a particular purpose, such as to discuss a business project or religious or community matters. For example, in March 1919 newspapers reported a 'large hui' planned in Gisborne to welcome Maori troops returning from England and the First World War. Another important form of hui is the tangi.

Tapu

Tapu means sacred or forbidden as a result of a religious or superstitious restriction. The term is commonly used in reference to burial grounds. The Maori tapu is similar to a Tongan word with the same meaning, which was heard by early European explorers and led to the English word taboo.

Pataka

Traditionally, Maori kept food and household equipment, including mats, baskets, clothing and fishing gear, in storehouses known as pataka. Such structures could be elaborately carved, and were raised above the ground on piles to protect their contents from rats. In 1998 the idea of a storehouse of treasures was adopted by the Porirua Museum, when it changed its name to Pataka Museum of Arts and Cultures.

Whare

A whare is a house. The word is also used to describe buildings with a special purpose, such as whare kai, where food is served on a marae and whare karakia — a church, chapel or house of prayer.

By the late nineteenth century the word 'whare' had been adopted by European settlers for small simple houses built to accommodate workmen on a farm, such as the shearers' quarters.

Maori Battalion

During the First World War New Zealand sent a Maori Pioneer Battalion, known as the Maori Battalion, to France. During the Second World War the companies of the 28 [Maori] Battalion were organised along tribal lines. The Maori Battalion served in North Africa, where Te Moana nui-a-Kiwa Ngarimu earned a Victoria Cross, as well as in Greece, Crete and Italy.

The Maori Battalion is remembered by its own marching song, with the stirring chorus:

Maori Battalion march to victory
Maori Battalion staunch and true
Maori Battalion march to glory
Take the honour of the people with you
We will march, march, march to the enemy
And we'll fight right to the end.
For God! For King! And for Country!
AU E! Ake, ake, kia kaha e!

Tiki

The tiki — who in some Maori traditions is a god — was represented originally by large wooden carvings. The name tiki later referred to smaller carvings, in particular those known as hei tiki — highly prized greenstone ornaments worn around the neck that depict a stylised human figure. It is one of the most distinctive images of Maori culture.

Matariki

In recent years the celebration of Matariki, the traditional Maori new year, has become popular. It is marked, towards the end of May each year, by the appearance of a small cluster of stars — known to astronomers as Pleiades — that rise on the northeast horizon. To Maori this indicates the start of a new life cycle, and the new year is marked by the next new moon.

Maui

Maui is a figure who occurs in traditional legends from around the Pacific. According to New Zealand Maori, Maui was responsible for fishing up the North Island, which was named Te Ika a Maui — the Fish of Maui. His other feats included bringing fire to the world and slowing down the passage of the sun across the sky.

Kupe

In Maori legend Kupe is said to have sailed from Hawaiki to discover New Zealand. He then returned to his legendary homeland

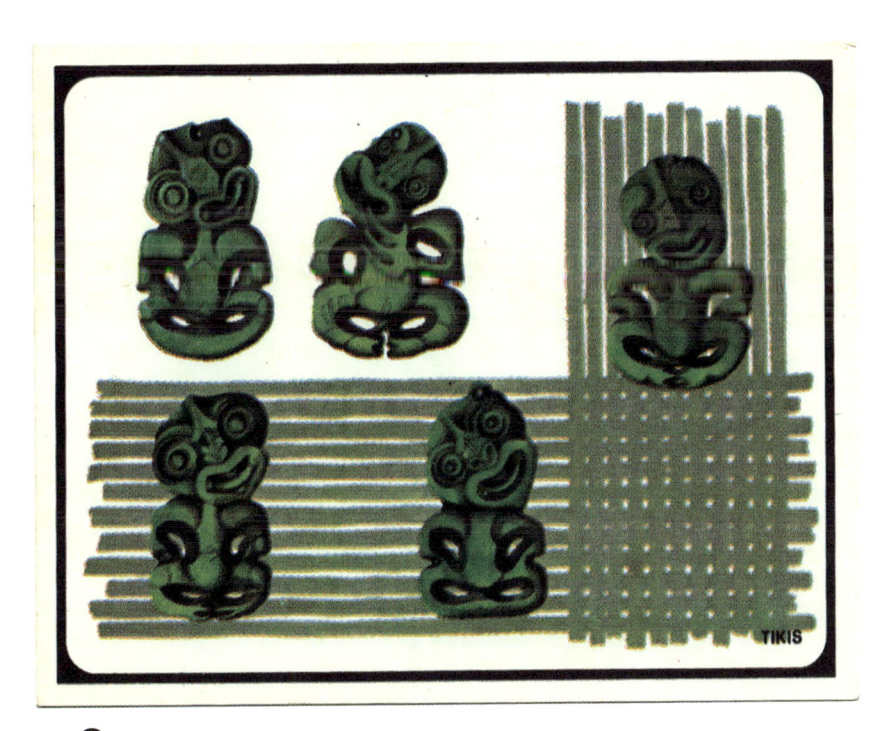

Five representations of the distinctive greenstone Maori tiki.

Tangata WHENUA 155

and, following his directions, other Polynesians were able to make the journey.

Taniwha

The taniwha is a mythical monster of Maori legend that lived in rivers, lakes and the ocean. In 1850 a European explorer in the Matamata district had to cross a number of swamps, one of which was said by Maori to be 'infested by a very wicked taniwha called Rito'. Apparently this monster enjoyed eating Pakeha, whom he dragged under the water and ate, bones and all, at the bottom of the swamp.

Another taniwha, a one-eyed monster known as Kahu Tahi, was in the news in 2002. His home, in a small swamp near the Meremere power station, lay in the way of planned improvements to State Highway 1. Negotiations were required between road builders and local Maori before the roadworks could be completed.

Hikoi

The term 'hikoi', meaning a march by a group of people in support of a cause, became popular following the march to Waitangi by Maori protesters in 1984. In late 2004 another hikoi from Northland arrived in Wellington to protest at the Government's foreshore and seabed legislation.

Perhaps the earliest and best known hikoi was the 1975 Maori Land March led by Dame Whina Cooper, from Cape Reinga to Parliament in Wellington, where they presented a petition to

Parliament. The Waitangi Tribunal was established later that year for the purpose of hearing grievances against the Crown over breaches of the Treaty of Waitangi. Two years later Maori and pakeha marched in protest against plans to build luxury housing on Bastion Point in Orakei, Auckland.

Te Maori

A taonga is a highly prized or culturally valuable object. Translated it means 'treasure'. The word was frequently used in reference to the collection of carved wooden and stone treasures included in the successful *Te Maori* exhibition, which was shown in three international venues (including the prestigious Metropolitan Museum of Art in New York) in 1984. *Te Maori* then returned to New Zealand and undertook a tour of major museums and art galleries.

Kapai

Kapai — meaning good or excellent — has enjoyed general use for a long time. For example, in the early twentieth century it was a popular brand name, for boots and brooms. In 1843, following a clash between Maori and European settlers, Te Rauparaha was reported as saying: 'Kapai the korero, no good the fight.'

— *New Zealand Gazette and Wellington Spectator*, 2 September 1843

Pakeha

The Maori word for a non-Maori person is Pakeha. It was first used in the nineteenth century, and its origin is unknown. Today the majority of New Zealanders of European ancestry consider their ethnicity to be Pakeha New Zealander.

Maoriland

In the late nineteenth century New Zealand had several alternative names, mostly used by Romantic poets and writers. One such name was Maoriland. The people who lived in Maoriland were called Maorilanders.

Godzone
COUNTRY

New Zealand

Dutch geographers gave New Zealand its name in the seventeenth century after Abel Tasman — the first known European to see New Zealand — named it Staten Landt: Land of the [Dutch] States-General, in 1642. Tasman thought it might be connected to South America, which had been given that same name earlier. When it was found the two land masses were not linked the islands to the west were named Nieuw Zeeland, which honoured the maritime province of Zeeland in Holland. The name became anglicised to New Zealand.

National anthem

New Zealand has the unusual claim of two national anthems. The first, 'God Save the Queen', was the official anthem in 1840 when New Zealand became a British colony. Irish-born Thomas Bracken, this country's most popular poet, wrote 'God Defend New Zealand' in 1870, and music was provided by John Joseph Woods, a schoolteacher from Lawrence, Otago. The song gained in popularity and in 1940, New Zealand's centennial year, it was declared the national hymn. 'God Save the Queen' remained the national anthem until 1977 when, following a petition, the government gave 'God Defend New Zealand' equal status. It is now the more popular of the two anthems and is usually played, with Maori words, at international sporting events.

National flag

New Zealand's first flag was chosen by a group of Maori chiefs in 1834. Known as the flag of the United Tribes of New Zealand, it consisted of a St George's Cross, and four stars on a blue field in the top left-hand quarter. The flag was used by ships, and on land for a period after the signing of the Treaty of Waitangi (after which the British Union Jack was adopted as a national flag), and is still used by various Maori groups.

In 1867 the colony's ships began using a flag known as the Blue Ensign. The design included the Union Jack, with the Southern Cross (see page 280) represented by four five-pointed stars. With modifications, it was officially adopted as the national flag or ensign in 1901, following patriotism associated with this country's involvement in the South African War.

The existing ensign has been criticised for its similarity to the Australian flag, for its British and colonial overtones, and its lack of reference to Maori culture. One of the most popular alternative flags for New Zealand was the 'Koru' design by Austrian artist Friedensreich Hundertwasser in 1983.

Dominion

On 26 September 1907 the Colony of New Zealand became the Dominion of New Zealand by royal proclamation of King Edward VII. It was really a change in name only. On that day New Zealand became a dominion within the British Empire, as did Newfoundland, following Canada in 1867 and Australia in 1901. The Union of South Africa also became a dominion in 1910.

There is also a long straight road, running from Eden Terrace through Balmoral to Mount Roskill in Auckland, made famous by the Muttonbirds' song 'Dominion Road'.

Godzone COUNTRY

Coat of arms

In 1911, four years after it had become a dominion, New Zealand held a competition to select a national coat of arms. The winning design featured a European woman — Zealandia — holding the national flag, and a Maori warrior wielding a taiaha. Between the pair was a shield decorated with the Southern Cross and references to New Zealand's main economic activities, including shipping, mining and sheepfarming. In 1956 this official coat of arms was updated; Zealandia and the Maori warrior now stand on fronds of fern and are turned to face one another.

National symbols

The country's official national symbols include the Southern Cross (see page 280), which is seen on both the flag and the coat of arms, and the silver fern (see page 164), which was added to the coat of arms in 1956. The popular kiwi is not an official national symbol.

The black jersey

New Zealand's preference for black began with the jerseys worn by its national rugby team in the 1880s, even before the name All Blacks had been adopted. Since then, most national sports teams have worn black. Black has, therefore, become associated with intense patriotism. The colour has also been adopted by other sporting codes in the team names, including the Black Caps in cricket and Black Sticks in hockey. New Zealand's successful bid for the America's Cup was in a boat named *Black Magic*.

New Zealand's official national coat of arms, a 1956 update of the original 1911 design.

Godzone COUNTRY

Silver fern

The silver fern is one of our national emblems and led to New Zealanders during the First World War being referred to as Fernleaves. Fernleaf is a well-known brand of butter. Our national netball team is known as the Silver Ferns.

Waitangi Day

On 6 February every year New Zealand has a national holiday to mark the signing of the Treaty of Waitangi in 1840. The day was first officially commemorated in 1934, although it did not become an acknowledged anniversary until 1960. From 1974 it became a national public holiday; the day was renamed New Zealand Day in 1975 but quickly reverted to Waitangi Day the following year.

The ANZACs

On 25 April 1915 Australian and New Zealand troops landed at Gallipoli, on the Dardanelles Peninsula, Turkey. They soon became known as the ANZACs — an acronym for Australian and New Zealand Army Corps. Later, the beach where the men landed was named Anzac Cove. The term ANZAC was used for all Australian and New Zealand troops who took part in the campaign on the Dardanelles, and also applied to combined forces from those two countries during other campaigns in the First World War, as well as in the Second World War and Vietnam.

Soon after the disastrous experience at Gallipoli the word Anzac was used for a wide range of commercial products and, as a result, in 1916, it was protected by law from exploitation.

ANZAC Day

Following receipt of news of the dramatic landing of ANZAC troops at Gallipoli, a half-day holiday was declared in New Zealand. In 1922 the public need for a form of remembrance, both as an expression of grief and patriotism, led to the official declaration of 25 April as a full public holiday

ANZAC Day honours New Zealanders killed in all wars, with the commemorations usually involving a pre-dawn march by returned service personnel to their local war memorial hall or monument (see page 168). A short service includes prayers and hymns, and finishes with the last verse of Laurence Binyon's poem 'For the Fallen':

They shall not grow old, as we that are left grow old:
Age shall not weary them, nor the years condemn.
At the going down of the sun and in the morning
We will remember them.

ANZAC Day ceremonies attracted large attendances during the Second World War and the 1950s, while following decades saw the day become associated with protest at war-related issues. But the seventy-fifth anniversary of the landings at Gallipoli in 1990 saw a growth of public interest in marking ANZAC Day. In the last few years, significant numbers of young New Zealanders and Australians on their OE have made a pilgrimage to attend the dawn service at Gallipoli on 25 April.

The ANZAC Day dawn parade — a combined services ceremony — acknowledges that New Zealand soldiers (along with their Australian allies) went ashore at Gallipoli at dawn on 25 April 1915.

Poppy Day

The annual Poppy Day Appeal in New Zealand goes back to 1922. Originally a French idea, it was first held here on 24 April, the day before ANZAC Day. The sale of artificial poppies by the RSA raises funds for the care of the country's returned service personnel and their families. It continues to be a popular national event.

> *The RSA's annual Poppy Day Appeal, which coincides with ANZAC Day, raises money for New Zealand's returned service personnel and their families.*

Digger

New Zealand and Australian soldiers in the First World War were known as diggers. The term had been in popular use in both countries prior to the war, applied to miners and, in New Zealand, to gumdiggers. It seems that as soldiers needed to dig trenches they were called diggers. At Gallipoli the ANZAC soldiers were known as diggers, although, in time, the New Zealanders were also referred to as Kiwis.

J-force

J-force, or Jayforce, was the New Zealand contribution to a Commonwealth force sent to Japan following its defeat on 15 August

1945. The New Zealanders were involved in searching for military equipment, providing medical assistance and overseeing repatriation centres as the Japanese returned home. Altogether some 12,000 New Zealanders — including several hundred women — served with J-Force from 1945 to 1949.

Kayforce

The ground force New Zealand sent to the Korean War in the period from late 1950 to 1957 was known as Kayforce. A total of 3794 men served, of whom 33 were killed on active service.

Dinkum

Dinkum, implying quality or the real thing — most commonly used in the expression 'fair dinkum' — may come from an old English word dink, which means trim or neat. During the First World War, members of the New Zealand Rifle Brigade became known as the Dinkums, or Dinks, which was a reference to their standards and sense of patriotism. Today, fair dinkum is more commonly observed in Aussie vernacular.

RSA

the New Zealand Returned Soldiers' Association, formed in 1916, was renamed the New Zealand Returned Services' Association (RSA) during the Second World War. The name change recognised the war service of the New Zealand naval and air forces and the mercantile marine. In 2004 the organisation was renamed the Royal New Zealand Returned and Services' Association. The RSA and its branch associations raise funds to carry out social and welfare work to assist needy ex-servicemen and their families.

Today there are more than 170 RSAs around the country and 135,000 active members. These days you don't need to be a war veteran to become a member. Many Kiwis, young and old, enjoy going along to their local RSA for a pub meal, a cheap drink and to watch sport on large-screen TVs.

War memorials

A distinctive feature of New Zealand's towns and cities, war memorials honour the large number of citizens who have died in conflicts around the world. The first war in which New Zealanders fought overseas took place in South Africa, in 1899–1902, which resulted in some 44 memorials around the country. The death of 18,166 New Zealand service personnel in the First World War gave rise to over 500 new monuments. After the Second World War, when another 11,625 New Zealand service personnel lost their lives, a different attitude to war memorials emerged. Instead of ornamental monuments, the country built living memorials in the form of community facilities, such as halls, sports grounds, libraries and swimming pools.

New Zealand's largest war memorial is the Auckland War Memorial Museum, completed in 1929 to honour Aucklanders who had died in the First World War. Thirty-one years later the museum gained an extension as a memorial to the Second World War.

Biculturalism

The idea of biculturalism, along with the promotion of Maori traditions and values, gathered momentum in New Zealand in the 1980s. Developments included encouraging Maori to speak te reo and have their own educational facilities, such as kohanga reo. Government departments gained equivalent Maori names, such as Ministry of Health Manatu Hauora and Inland Revenue Te Tari Taake. Biculturalism was also apparent in the approach taken by the Museum of New Zealand Te Papa Tongarewa, which opened in 1993.

Aotearoa

The origin of the Maori concept of Aotearoa is unclear, but is popularly taken to mean 'The Land of the Long White Cloud': ao/cloud, tea/white, and roa/long. According to some accounts, the explorer Kupe was first to give the name to this country. Early Maori use of the term referred to the North Island only, but from the nineteenth century European writers and historians applied the name to the whole of New Zealand, as in the title of William Pember Reeves' history of the country, *The Long White Cloud: Ao Tea Roa*, first published in 1898. Since then Aotearoa has been frequently used as an alternative to New Zealand; for example, in the Maori version of the national anthem (see page 160).

Godzone

In 1906 New Zealand Prime Minister Richard — King Dick — Seddon (see page 189) died on board ship while returning from Australia. Before departing he sent a telegram to the Premier of Victoria advising: 'Just leaving for God's own country'. This reference to New Zealand was also used by Thomas Bracken as the name of one of his poems. 'God's own country' was later shortened to Godzone.

Old Country

Until the mid-1900s New Zealanders referred to the Old Country that they had left to come here — usually it was Britain. It was similar to 'home', and writer Samuel Butler used both expressions in one paragraph in 1860 when comparing life in New Zealand with that back in England. He wondered whether 'the intellect is not as well schooled here as at home', but observed there was 'much nonsense in the old country from which people here are free'.

Sir Edmund Hillary

Sir Edmund Hillary is one of the best known New Zealanders in the world. Born in Auckland in 1919, he was knighted in 1953 after conquering Everest. He later became involved with the British Trans-Antarctic Expedition, and made the first overland trip to the South Pole with vehicles in 1958. On many occasions he returned to the Himalayan region to promote the building of hospitals and schools for the Sherpa people, and from 1985 to 1989 he served as New Zealand High Commissioner in New Delhi, India. In a 2007 *Listener* readers' poll Sir Ed was voted the most admired New Zealander. He died in 2008.

Sir Ernest Rutherford

Ernest Rutherford was born near Nelson in 1871 and became the greatest physicist of his day. After studying at Nelson College and

Canterbury University he became a research student at the Cavendish Laboratory, Cambridge, England and, later, professor at universities in Montreal and Manchester. In 1913 he developed a theory to explain the particles that make up the atom, and his pioneering work paved the way for the atomic age. Rutherford was knighted in 1914 and became Baron Rutherford of Nelson in 1931. He was awarded honorary doctorates from 21 universities around the world. He died in 1937 and was interred in Westminster Abbey.

Captain Charles Upham, VC and Bar

Charles Upham is the only combat soldier to be awarded the Victoria Cross twice. Born in Christchurch in 1908, he served during the Second World War in Greece, and later in Crete where he was wounded in the shoulder. As a result of the exceptional gallantry he had shown in Crete he was awarded the Victoria Cross. He next saw action in North Africa, where he was more seriously wounded. When his company was overrun by German tanks he was taken prisoner and sent to a camp in Italy. Following his increasingly daring attempts to escape he was transferred to a special camp at Colditz, in Germany, where he remained, reluctantly, until the end of the war. It was later decided that Upham's actions in North Africa were worthy of the highest recognition possible and, so, he received a bar to his Victoria Cross. He died in 1994.

GUMMINT

Governor-General

When New Zealand became a British colony in 1840, the sovereign — then Queen Victoria — became Head of State and had a representative in this country. The first was Captain William Hobson, who was Lieutenant-Governor and, later, Governor. In 1848 the position became Governor-in-Chief, and in 1853 Governor of the self-governing Colony of New Zealand. In 1917 the title became Governor-General, and 19 individuals have held the post since.

The Maori Wars

Until the late twentieth century, the previous century's conflicts between Maori and Pakeha were commonly known as the Maori Wars. This was a European view of what are now most often referred to as the New Zealand Wars.

The New Zealand Wars

The New Zealand Wars took place between the 1840s and 1872 and were a series of clashes between various North Island Maori tribes and British and colonial forces. This period is now also referred to as The Land Wars.

First past the post

From 1853 New Zealand elections were based on the first-past-the-post — FPP — electorate-based system. Each voter had one vote and the candidate receiving the most votes was the winner, becoming Member of Parliament for their electorate. Under this system the successful

Her Majesty Queen Elizabeth II contemplating the weather in Blenheim on a 1977 visit to New Zealand.

174 Crikey!

political party usually won a greater share of seats than its share of overall votes. It encouraged strong single-party governments and disadvantaged smaller parties. In 1993 New Zealanders voted to change from FPP to an MMP or mixed-member-proportional voting system.

Royal visits

New Zealand received its first visit from a member of British royalty in April 1869 when Queen Victoria's second son — Prince Alfred, the Duke of Edinburgh — arrived in Wellington on the first of three trips to this country. The first visit from a reigning monarch began on 23 December 1953 when Queen Elizabeth II and the Duke of Edinburgh arrived in Auckland. By the time the royal couple departed from Bluff on 30 January 1954 they had visited 46 towns and cities and attended 110 separate functions. They had travelled some 2100 kilometres by car, 1160 by air and 970 by train around the country.

Another memorable royal visit was that of Prince Charles, Prince of Wales, and Diana, Princess of Wales, and their son, Prince William, in 1983. It was Charles' fifth visit to this country.

Continuance

Widespread public drunkenness in nineteenth century New Zealand led to a strong prohibition movement, which campaigned to ban the sale of liquor altogether. From the 1890s polls gave voters the chance to choose between the continuing public sale of liquor in their district (continuance), prohibition, or state control.

THE SUMMIT AT LAST.

In 1893, 60 years before Edmund Hillary reached the summit of Mount Everest, Zealandia scaled the lofty 'Parliamentary Heights' and finally achieved votes for New Zealand women.

176 Crikey!

These polls were held every three years from 1911 to 1987 inclusive (except 1931 and 1951) in conjunction with the general election. The last three districts to remain 'dry' were Mount Eden, Mount Roskill and Tawa, which all became wet in 1999.

Votes for Women

In 1893 New Zealand became the first country in the world to grant women the right to vote in parliamentary elections. Women were already entitled to vote in certain parts of the United States, and the British colony of Pitcairn Island, but New Zealand was the first self-governing nation to grant them the right. We beat Australia by nine years, and were even further ahead of Britain and the United States.

In 1891 and 1892 New Zealand's House of Representatives passed bills that would have given women the vote, but on both occasions they were defeated in the upper house of Parliament. A third attempt was successful, and on 8 September 1893 the bill was passed by 20 votes to 18.

The National Party

The National Party, one of the two dominant parties in modern New Zealand politics, was created in the mid-1930s. It promoted self-reliance, rejecting socialism and state control, and it first became government in 1949 under Prime Minister Sidney Holland. A more recent and more memorable National leader was Sir Robert Muldoon, who was Prime Minister from 1975 until 1984. His aggressive style, antagonistic, distinctive voice and characteristics made him an obvious target for cartoonists and comedians.

The Labour Party

The Labour Party has been one of the two primary political parties in New Zealand for the past 80 years. Growing from an organisation formed in 1910, the Labour Party gained its first seats in Parliament in 1919, and became the government for the first time in 1935 under Prime Minister Michael Joseph Savage (see page 188). Since then, Labour governments have been elected in 1957, 1972 and 1984, before Helen Clark led the fifth Labour Government to victory in 1999 and again in 2002 and 2005.

Social Credit

Social Credit was a monetary philosophy that led to the formation of a political party in 1953. The Social Credit Party began contesting the general elections from the following year and won a seat in 1966, which it held for one term. It also won a seat in 1978. The party enjoyed its greatest popularity in the early 1980s and in 1985 it changed its name to the Democratic Party.

Welfare state

The welfare state, in which the government provides assistance for less fortunate members of society, was an idea popularised in the 1930s. It was practised in a number of countries, particularly in Europe, as well as New Zealand. It gained momentum following the poverty of the Depression. In New Zealand the idea led to the Social Security Act 1938, brought in by the Labour government under Michael Joseph Savage. The act introduced a wide range of financial assistance opportunites for citizens, including medical, hospital and maternity benefits.

Social security and social welfare

Social security — now usually referred to as social welfare — is the basis of the welfare state. New Zealand's first achievement in this area was the passing of an old-age pension in 1898. As the idea developed, the Social Security Act 1938 was passed and the welfare state was maintained until the 1950s. Since then the introduction of free-market economic measures has seen the dismantling of parts of the original social security plan.

State Advances

In 1894 the New Zealand Government made loans available to farmers under what was known as the Advances to Settlers Act. Twelve years later an Advances to Workers Act enabled people on low incomes to buy their own homes. These two acts led to the creation of what became known in 1936 as the State Advances Corporation. In 1974 it merged with the Housing Division of the Ministry of Works to become the Housing Corporation of New Zealand. In 2001 the Housing Corporation merged with other government organisations to become Housing New Zealand.

Superannuation

In New Zealand the word super has two important and very different meanings, and in both cases it is an abbreviation. Super(annuation) is the old-age pension, originally brought in by the Liberal government under Richard Seddon in 1898, while super(phosphate) is a fertiliser (see page 214). Super(annuation) was the first of its kind in any British country, and is regarded as the beginnings of social security in New Zealand. This benefit continues today as the New Zealand Superannuation Fund and provides a retirement income for people aged 65 and over.

Florin

The florin was the nickname for the British two-shilling coin, which circulated from about 1850 to 1970. In 1935 New Zealand issued its own coinage, including a two-shilling florin featuring a kiwi. With the introduction of decimal currency in 1967 the New Zealand florin disappeared, replaced by a 20-cent coin that also featured a kiwi.

Decimal currency

The first suggestions that New Zealand should change to decimal currency — a system based on the number 10 — were made in 1880. Finally, on 10 July 1967 (known as DC Day) New Zealanders were able to get rid of their old pennies, threepences, sixpences, shillings and pounds. The old 10-bob or 10-shilling note was now worth $1, conveniently divided into 100 cents.

Income tax

In the late nineteenth century the New Zealand government relied on customs duties as its main source of both taxation and income. Taxes on land and income were introduced in 1891, and applied to all incomes above £300. The tax rate was 6d (sixpence) in the pound on the first taxable £1000, and 1/- (a shilling) in the pound on taxable incomes over £1000. Today, such taxes as income tax and GST are collected by the Department of Inland Revenue Te Tari Taake.

The country's successful conversion to decimal currency was overseen by Robert Muldoon, who later became Minister of Finance and Prime Minister of New Zealand.

Bonus bonds

Bonus bonds were introduced by the New Zealand government in 1970 in an attempt to encourage New Zealanders to save. Owners of bonds also had a chance to win extra cash, with over 200,000 cash prizes, including one of $1 million, in monthly prize draws. At first the bonus bond scheme was operated by the Post Office Savings Bank, which later became part of PostBank. Since 1990 the scheme has been administered by ANZ Investment Services (New Zealand).

Mr Dollar, worth 10 shillings in the old money, got to meet New Zealanders on DC Day, 10 July 1967.

Nuclear-free policy

The 1970s saw New Zealanders increasingly opposed to France's detonation of nuclear devices in the Pacific, and in 1973 the government sent the frigate HMNZS *Otago* to the Mururoa testing site in protest. New Zealand's growing anti-nuclear movement led to protests at visits by nuclear-powered warships from the United States, and a cooling of relations between the two countries. The anti-nuclear concept was further embraced by David Lange's Labour government in 1984. Two years later this country ratified the South Pacific Nuclear Free Zone Treaty, and in 1987 New Zealand's own Nuclear Free Zone, Disarmament and Arms Control Act came into force.

Rainbow Warrior

On 10 July 1985 the Greenpeace protest vessel *Rainbow Warrior* was blown up and sunk by French agents in Auckland Harbour, causing the death of a Greenpeace photographer. This act of international terrorism was in response to Greenpeace's campaign against nuclear weapons. Repairs were carried out to the ship but in 1987 it was towed to Matauri Bay, about 30 kilometres north of Kerikeri, where it was deliberately sunk. There is a *Rainbow Warrior* memorial sculpture at Matauri Bay and offshore the ship has become a popular attraction for divers.

Rogernomics

While Britons had Thatcherism and the Americans had Reaganism, New Zealanders had to put up with Rogernomics. This was a popular name for the free-market policies introduced by Roger Douglas — the Labour government's Minister of Finance from 1984 to 1988. His policies involved the dismantling and selling-off of many state assets, and the removal of subsidies and supports in the interests of creating a more competitive economy. Douglas's measures included the introduction of GST in 1986.

Members of CANWAR (Campaign Against Nuclear Warships) protest at the arrival of the USS Longbeach *in Wellington Harbour in 1976.*

SOEs

In the 1980s New Zealanders were introduced to the term SOE, which was short for State-owned Enterprise. SOEs were companies established by the government to manage its trading activities; these were now required to operate as successful commercial businesses. From 1986 the government began selling off some of its State-owned Enterprises, including Post Office Bank Ltd, New Zealand Shipping Company, New Zealand Steel Ltd, Government Printing Office,

National Film Unit, Tourist Hotel Corporation of New Zealand, and Bank of New Zealand. In 1987 the Government established 14 new SOEs and that number has grown. The current list covers four areas of activity: Energy (including Electricity Corporation of New Zealand Ltd, Genesis Power Ltd, Meridian Energy Ltd, and Transpower New Zealand Ltd); Land and Environment (including Landcorp Farming Ltd and Quotable Value Ltd), Science and Infrastructure (including Airways Corporation of New Zealand Ltd and Learning Media Ltd) and Communications (including New Zealand Post Ltd)

Family benefit

In 1938 the Labour government's new social security scheme included a universal family benefit, which was paid for every child under the age of 16 years. It could be extended to the age of 18 if required; for example, if a child was in full-time education. From April 1959 parents were able to capitalise on the family benefit by applying for an advance payment of up to £1000 to help buy a house. The family benefit was abolished in 1992.

Daylight saving

In summer the clocks in New Zealand are moved forward an hour to provide extra daylight in the evening. It is known as daylight saving and was first suggested in the 1890s. There was resistance to the idea in rural areas, so it was not brought in until 1927. This only lasted for one year. In 1928 another Act was passed ruling that clocks would only go forward half an hour at the start of the summer, making this country 12 hours ahead of Greenwich Mean Time. In 1941 daylight saving was continued throughout the whole year due to emergency regulations. In

1974 new legislation ruled that daylight saving would be a one-hour advance on New Zealand Standard Time. It was adopted each year since then, and the daylight saving period was extended in 1989 and again in 2007 to a period of 27 weeks. Daylight saving begins on the last Sunday in September, when the clock is moved forward one hour, from 2.00 am to 3.00 am, and ends on the first Sunday in the following April when the clock is returned from 3.00 am to 2.00 am.

Capital cities

Wellington is New Zealand's third capital. After signing the Treaty of Waitangi in 1840 Governor William Hobson established the first capital at Okiato, across the channel from Opua in the Bay of Islands. He named it Russell after Lord Russell, Secretary of State for the colonies and, later, Prime Minister of Britain. In 1841 Hobson shifted his seat of government to Auckland, and three years later the name Russell was officially transferred to the nearby settlement of Kororareka. Today Okiato is sometimes referred to as 'Old Russell'.

In 1865 the seat of government was transferred from Auckland to Wellington. That city has the distinction of being the southernmost capital city in the world.

King Country

The region of the central North Island between Te Awamutu and Taupo is known as the King Country because it was under the control of the Maori King, Tawhiao, and home to the King Movement in the late nineteenth century. The main towns in the region are Otorohanga,

Te Kuiti and Taumarunui. The King Country is not usually marked on maps, but has been in the name of a rugby union since 1922.

CER

The New Zealand–Australia free-trade agreement was signed on 1 January 1983. Known as Closer Economic Relations or, more simply, CER, it was designed to reduce import and export duties between the two countries. Free trade in goods and nearly all services was achieved by 1990.

Hobson's choice

Having Hobson's choice means you do not have a choice. The expression originated in England in the early 1600s. However, the first Lieutenant-Governor of the new colony of New Zealand was Captain William Hobson and, as a result, the expression took on a new meaning here. For example, Hobson's choice was used to refer to his choice of Auckland instead of Wellington as capital, and Nelson instead of Canterbury as a site for settlement.

Sesqui

In 1990 New Zealand marked its sesquicentennial— 150 years of European settlement since the signing of the Treaty of Waitangi. The Wellington festival — known as Sesqui — was a financial failure, with poor public attendance at events, and as a result 'sesqui' came to imply mismanagement and incompetence.

MMP

At a referendum associated with the 1993 general election, New Zealand voters decided to replace the existing first-past-the-post political system (fpp, also known as SMP — single-member-plurality) with mixed-member-proportional representation — MMP. Under this new system political parties would receive a share of seats in Parliament according to their share of the total votes cast. This country's first government formed under MMP was in 1996, and was a coalition between the National Party and New Zealand First.

Jo MacKay with her own pro-MMP billboard, 1993.

GUMMINT

Eight-hour day

The idea of an eight-hour working day was introduced to New Zealand in 1840 by London carpenter Samuel Duncan Parnell (not the Parnell after whom the Auckland suburb was named). New Zealand was the first country in the world to take up the idea. It was established nationally on a five-day 40-hour week basis in 1936, but since the 1980s the eight-hour working day is less common as a result of reduced union influence, individual work agreements between employers and employees, and a growing number of self-employed people.

Labour Day

The fourth Monday in October each year is a public holiday known as Labour Day. It commemorates the workers' struggle for an eight-hour day, and was first celebrated on 28 October 1890.

Michael Joseph Savage

Michael Joseph Savage was the first Labour Prime Minister, from 1935 until he died in 1940. He was a kindly, genial and much-loved figure. His photograph was displayed on many mantelpieces throughout the country. Savage was born in Australia and came to New Zealand in 1907. He joined the Labour Party when it was formed in 1916, and three years later he was elected to Parliament, representing Auckland West. He held the seat for the rest of his life, and in 1933 he became leader of the Labour Party. Two years later he was Prime Minister, and in 1938 he introduced his greatest achievement — the Social Security Bill. Savage is still considered one of the most popular of all this country's previous prime ministers.

King Dick

Richard Seddon — commonly known as King Dick — is the longest-serving Prime Minister in New Zealand's history. He held the post for 13 years and one month. He was born in Lancashire in 1845 and at the age of 18 he emigrated to Australia. After an unsuccessful period on the goldfields of Victoria he came across to Hokitika, in the South Island. He entered local politics in 1874, becoming a cabinet minister in 1891, and two years later he led the Liberal Party to victory in the general election. A tall and powerfully built man, he had a large public profile and autocratic manner that earned him the name King Dick. He was Premier and Prime Minister until 10 June 1906, when he died at sea while returning from Sydney to Wellington.

Number-eight WIRE

Early houses

The earliest surviving house built for Europeans in New Zealand belonged to J. Kemp and was built in Kerikeri, in the Bay of Islands, in 1819. As settlement spread, the typical timber houses — mostly two-room cottages — developed into larger villas and, from about 1918, California Bungalows (see page 194) began to dominate the towns and cities. The country's housing stock was extended with the State Housing scheme in the 1930s, and the last 50 years have seen increasing diversity in design and construction.

Typical Kiwi house

A 1997 survey aiming to determine the typical New Zealand house discovered it had three bedrooms, timber framing and a corrugated iron roof. However, North Island houses are more likely to be clad in fibre-cement panels or weatherboards than traditional wooden weatherboards. In the South Island, houses are more likely to be clad in brick veneer built on a solid concrete base. The typical New Zealand roof is now clad with pre-painted steel sheets rather than unpainted corrugated iron. Exterior window and door frames are likely to be of powder-coated aluminum.

State housing

The government began providing houses for New Zealanders in 1905 when Prime Minister Richard Seddon passed the Workers' Dwellings Act — with the first houses built for workers in Petone. More followed in the other main centres, but the programme folded in 1919. After the First World War the Railways Department began

A row of tiled-roof state houses in Mahoe Street, in the Lower Hutt suburb of Waterloo.

building suburbs of cottages for its workers around the country. Following the Depression, the first Labour Government, under Michael Joseph Savage, began a busy programme of state-house building — the first was completed in Miramar, Wellington, in 1937. Within two years there were 5000 of these new homes, and after the Second World War the Government was building some 10,000 state houses a year.

In the early 1950s large state housing areas were created in south Auckland and Porirua, north of Wellington. The National government of the 1990s sold off some of the state-housing stock, and only people on welfare could now rent a state home, but in 1999 the Labour government reinstated income-related rents.

Leaky homes

In the 1990s a large number of New Zealanders discovered they were living with what became known as leaky homes syndrome. Their dwellings had been built according to recently introduced construction methods which, during wet weather, allowed water to intrude and become trapped. Combined with the use of untreated timber, this could cause rotting and severe damage to the structure of the house, while the growth of moulds on damp timber could also result in breathing and skin problems for the occupants.

Villa

The villa — including square, single- and double-bay villas — is the type of house found in the older inner suburbs of most New Zealand cities and in rural towns throughout the country. The style was popular in the period from 1895 to 1910 and now represents an important part of our social and architectural heritage. The houses reflected the rising success and taste of the Victorian and Edwardian periods, with their emphasis on home and family. They were spacious, built of kauri, and richly decorated with ornamental fretwork. The front of the villa invariably faced the street. The first, smaller, villas were simple square buildings and a single-bay villa had a bay window on one side with a verandah on the other. The grander homes had two bay windows with a verandah between.

Bungalow

By the late 1910s, the most popular type of house built in New Zealand was the bungalow or California bungalow, a style imported from the west coast of the United States. These new houses replaced the previously popular villa, and typically had a lower roof. They were simpler than the villa, with fewer decorative features. They had casement and fanlight windows in place of the older houses' double-hung sash windows. They usually had built-in furniture and the luxury of an inside toilet and bathroom.

Sausage flats

In the 1960s and 1970s long rows of single- and double-storeyed blocks of flats began to appear in New Zealand cities due to a demand for affordable housing. They were usually of brick-and-tile construction, and because of their sausage-like shape became known as sausage flats.

Weatherboards

Weatherboards were the usual lining for the outside of early timber buildings in New Zealand. The idea of horizontally overlapping boards nailed onto a timber frame came here via Australia during the very early years of settlement. For example, an 1844 report about the home of the Deans brothers, two early Canterbury settlers, describes an 'excellent weather-board verandah house, with large and substantial out-buildings, and surrounded with abundance of the comforts and necessaries, as well as many of the luxuries of life'.

Four-by-two

New Zealanders are said to be able to make, or repair, anything with a bit of number-eight wire and a length of four-by-two [timber]. This was the standard-sized timber — four inches wide and two inches deep — used for framing in house construction. The same size is still used, now metricated to 100 millimetres by 50 millimetres.

The four-by-two is well-known in the United Kingdom and Australia as well as New Zealand, but in the United States the same-sized timber is referred to as a two-by-four.

Fibrolite

Fibrolite was a brand name for a range of building materials made of a mixture of cement and asbestos fibres. It was manufactured here by James Hardie & Co. Panels were rot-proof and borer-proof and were a cheap cladding, which quickly became popular for sheds and baches. Modern cement sheets no longer contain asbestos.

Number-eight WIRE

Pinex

Pinex is a brand name for a range of goods made from wood. In the 1960s it was applied to various types of composite panels, and was often used as the name for a soft wall lining — also known as insulating board — that was often used in baches (or cribs). The soft board was ideal for pin-up boards, too.

Corrugated iron

First produced in Britain in the 1830s and only considered suitable for temporary buildings at the time, corrugated iron is a building material that was quickly favoured for use in New Zealand. Known simply as iron, it is still widely used for roofs, sheds and water tanks.

In 1983 New Zealand writer Geoff Chapple described the 'unremitting ripple' of corrugated iron in this country, and how it had been 'slapped together for beach baches, for temporary fences which linger, for dog shelters you couldn't dignify with the name kennel . . .' However, the most unusual and elegant use for corrugated iron in New Zealand is by sculptor Jeff Thomson whose wonderful creations, ranging from herds of elephants to flocks of chooks, are in public and private collections all over the world.

Gib board

Gibraltar board — usually known as gib board — was first produced in 1927 in an Auckland factory that was later bought by Winstone Ltd. Changes to what was then known as Winstone Board saw

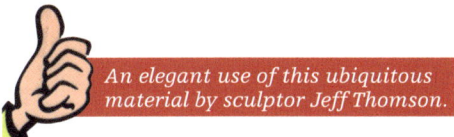

An elegant use of this ubiquitous material by sculptor Jeff Thomson.

Number-eight WIRE 197

New Zealand pumice — a light porous lava stone — replace sawdust at the core of the material. The pumice was mixed with gypsum and sandwiched between two layers of cardboard. Advertising boasted the new material was 'as solid as the rock of Gibraltar'.

The installation of gib board — nailing it onto timber framing — is known as gibbing. The specialist job of plastering over nail-heads and filling gaps between adjacent panels is called gib-stopping. The person who does the gib-stopping is called a gib-stopper.

Scoria

Scoria is a dark-red rock produced by the rapid cooling of lava flows from volcanoes. It is found throughout New Zealand, particularly in Auckland, where many of the region's original lava cones have been quarried to provide raw material for roads and building works.

A new settler described the first house she and her husband bought in their new home, Auckland, as being built of 'rough, unhewn scoria stone, plastered and whitewashed within; the roof is thatched with raupo, a kind of reed, of which the natives form their huts. The flooring is sound, and the roof not low. The interior area of the entire mansion measures exactly twenty feet by ten, but, by means of a curtain, is divided into an eating and sleeping apartment; these, in their time, play many parts; dining-room, drawing-room, boudoir, kitchen, nursery, library, and study.'

— *New Zealand Gazette and Wellington Spectator*, 10 December 1842; *New Zealander*, 22 September 1852

Ministry of Works

In 1870 the Public Works Department was formed to build the nation's roads, railways and other major construction projects. It became the Ministry of Works (MOW) in 1943 and continued to undertake most of the major construction work in the country, including roads and power stations. From 1984, following the reform of government departments the MOW, as such, disappeared and state projects could now be undertaken by private companies.

Grafton Bridge

In 1886 James Wilson & Co. of Warkworth, north of Auckland, were the first to produce locally made cement in commercial quantities. By then, local engineers were already exploring the possibilities of a new idea from overseas — reinforced concrete. This technique enabled Auckland's Grafton Bridge, which opened in 1910, to leap gracefully across Grafton Gully. Spanning 97.6 metres, it was the largest single-span of reinforced concrete in the world, and is believed to hold the record for the southern hemisphere.

Grafton Bridge was once notorious for the high number of suicides that took place there. The erection of barriers in 2003 has proved an effective deterrent.

Auckland Harbour Bridge

Until it became overshadowed by the Sky Tower, Auckland's Harbour Bridge probably qualified as the city's most recognisable man-made structure. Known as the coathanger for obvious reasons — another humorous nickname, inspired by traffic congestion, is 'car-strangled spanner' — the 1020-metre bridge connects St Mary's Bay with Northcote, on the North Shore. A week before the official opening on 30 May 1959, 106,500 people took the opportunity to walk across it. Some pedestrians required treatment by St John Ambulance for blisters and dozens of hats were blown off during the journey. One intoxicated citizen, in possession of a bottle of sherry and a cold pie, had the distinction of being the first person to be arrested on the bridge.

Toll booths were installed at the northern end of the bridge and it cost 2/6 (2 shillings and sixpence) or 25 cents per car to cross from south to north. This was later reduced to 2/- or 20 cents. The toll booths were closed in 1984.

Because of the rapid growth of Auckland's North Shore, the four-laned bridge was widened with another four lanes in 1969, affectionately known as the 'Nippon clip-ons' due to the fact they were designed and manufactured in Japan. The bridge can cope with some 180,000 vehicles per day, but it now seems likely a further harbour crossing — possibly a multi-tunnel link — will be needed to cope with Auckland's growing population.

The Beehive

One of the most important buildings in New Zealand is the Executive Wing of Parliament in Wellington, otherwise known as the Beehive. The 14-storey circular building houses the cabinet offices and the Prime Minister's department. The distinctive circular shape was the result of a sketch made in 1964 by visiting British architect Sir Basil Spence that,

A statue of New Zealand's longest serving prime minister, Richard 'King Dick' Seddon, stands in front of the Beehive, under construction.

Number-eight WIRE 201

according to rumour, was inspired by the image on a box of Beehive matches. Construction began in 1970 and it was finished in 1981.

Think Big

As a result of the international oil crisis in the early 1980s, New Zealand's National government under Robert Muldoon began an ambitious programme of large-scale construction projects. Known collectively as Think Big, the schemes were designed to save the country money by using local resources, including a plant at Waitara, in Taranaki, to convert natural gas from the Maui field into petrol, and the Clyde Dam on the Clutha River, in Central Otago, to generate electricity.

Hydro-electricity

New Zealand's fast-flowing rivers lend themselves perfectly to producing hydro-electricity. The first recorded instance of hydro-electric power usage was at Reefton, on the west coast of the South Island, in 1888. The first state-owned hydro-electric power station opened at Lake Coleridge in 1914, and other stations followed in the North Island. The bulk of the country's electricity was generated by these hydro schemes, but in 1958 the State Hydro-Electric Department was renamed the New Zealand Electricity Department, reflecting the fact that electricity was now being produced by other means.

Town icons and 'big things'

In the 1980s, as New Zealand's population drifted to the cities, small towns began to promote their attractions. They used a range of devices, including signs, murals and constructions of large objects with a local flavour. The idea of these roadside 'big things', or town icons, began in the United States during the Depression, and then spread to Australia and, eventually, New Zealand.

One of New Zealand's earliest and best-known town icons is the tribute to the locally produced soft drink, Lemon & Paeroa (see page 58). A number of other towns have also built monuments, including Riverton's four-metre tall paua, Gore's 6.5-metre tall trout, Rakaia's 12 metre tall salmon, Ohakune's nine-metre tall carrot, Te Puke's slice of kiwifruit, Cromwell's bunch of fruit, Te Kuiti's sheep shearer, and Tirau's corrugated-iron sheep.

Chippies and sparkies

In New Zealand a carpenter is commonly referred to as a chippie, the term originating in Britain and no doubt inspired by wood chips. By a similar logic, an electrician is known as a sparkie.

A building contractor employs different specialists, such as electricians, plumbers and painters, who are known as subbies — which is derived from sub-contractor.

Cow COCKIES

Cows

The first cattle to arrive in New Zealand were two cows and a bull brought to the Bay of Islands by Samuel Marsden in 1814. The earliest herds were mostly shorthorns, which provided meat as well as milk for butter and cheese. The first Jersey cows arrived in 1862, followed by Friesians and Ayrshires.

Cowsheds and herringbone sheds

An essential building on a New Zealand dairy farm is the cowshed, or milking shed, where twice-daily milking takes place. The early cowsheds were of various designs, including the race, the double bail, the single back-out and the walk through.

In 1952, following the development of milking machines, Ron Sharp, a Waikato farmer, designed the herringbone shed in which cows are angle-parked in two rows on either side of the milking-machine operators. The space-saving layout made the twice-daily job much easier, and reduced the distance the operator needed to travel. The idea quickly caught on and became the industry standard.

Dairy farming

By 1960 New Zealand could claim it produced the greatest annual quantity of dairy produce in the world per head of population, and until recently it led the world in annual quantities of cheese exported. In 2002 New Zealand had 14,000 farms with dairy cattle compared with 13,000 sheep farms. Waikato and Taranaki are the country's main dairying regions, although in recent years Canterbury has enjoyed the greatest increase in dairy cattle numbers.

Sharemilking

Sharemilking began in New Zealand in the early 1900s to enable young farmers to get a start in the dairy industry. The owner of a farm who provided land, buildings, stock and machinery would come to a profit-sharing agreement with the sharemilker, who would live on the farm and provide all the labour. The sharemilker was likely to be a married man who was assisted in his farm work by members of his family. As a step up the ladder to farm ownership, sharemilkers would first buy a herd, then source a sharemilking agreement with a retired farmer who provided land, buildings and machinery. By 1930 there were said to be hundreds of either retired or active farmers in Taranaki who, beginning as sharemilkers, had been able to save enough to buy their own herds of cows and, later, their own farms.

Cow-pat

A mound of cow manure — hence the need for gumboots on farms!

Bobby calf

Young calves aged between four days and three months old, usually male, are known as bobby calves. They are sent to the freezing works and the meat is sold as boneless veal. The New Zealand bobby-calf industry began as a result of the demand for rennet — needed for the production of cheese. Rennet is extracted from the stomach of young calves.

A dairy farm worker enjoys the benefits of the herringbone layout for the milking shed.

Cow COCKIES 207

Dog trials

The important job done by dogs on the sheep farms of New Zealand has developed into the recognised sport of dog trialling. The first trials were held in South Canterbury in 1889, followed by a competition in the North Island three years later. In the competitions the dogs undergo tasks similar to those they are required to perform on the farm. A national association was formed in 1957.

Header

Header dogs are trained to head off stock and drive them back towards their master. These dogs are quiet and careful workers, and have a natural instinct for rounding up sheep. In 1899 a shepherd described how he preferred a header to 'start at a fair pace, with head in the air and eye continually on the watch for the "quarry" . . . with head slightly to the side next the sheep, and eye only lifted off them when the ground compels him to pick his going'.

— *Otago Witness*, 9 November 1899

Huntaway

A huntaway dog works the sheep upwards and away from the master. An ideal dog for such duties is free-running and noisy, but able to obey commands. There are two types of huntaway competition — zig-zag and straight events.

Dog-dosing strips

Dog-dosing strips were once a feature of rural New Zealand. Dogs were treated at the dosing strips in an attempt to eradicate the hydatids tapeworm. Hydatids can infect other animals, including sheep, cattle and humans. A national council was set up in 1959 to deal with the problem and eventually, in 2002, New Zealand was declared free of hydatids. Dog-dosing strips were immortalised by Dunedin-born bandleader and recording artist Ken Avery in his song 'The Dog-dosing Strip at Dunsandel' — Dunsandel is a farming town on the Canterbury Plains.

Sheep

Sheep have long been central to the New Zealand economy. They were first introduced, although unsuccessfully, by Captain James Cook. Missionaries brought sheep here in the early 1800s, but the first real flock was established on Mana Island, offshore from Porirua Harbour near Wellington, in 1834. At first, sheep were farmed mainly for their wool and to supply locals with meat.

With the introduction of refrigerated shipping in 1882, New Zealand sheepfarmers had new opportunities. The most profitable sheep now provided the best possible wool as well as the best carcass for freezing.

Merino

The Merino originated in Spain and is the oldest established and most numerous sheep breed in the world. It was first brought to New

New Zealand's most economically important animal, the sheep, was honoured on this postage stamp in 1982.

Zealand in sizeable numbers in the 1830s and was our dominant breed until the early 1900s. It produces fine wool, and there are currently some 2.5 million Merinos in this country.

Probably New Zealand's best known Merino is a hermit ram named after the green ogre in the animated film *Shrek*. Living in mountain caves in Central Otago, the ram avoided the annual muster for six years — until 2004. Finally recaptured, he became an instant celebrity and was shorn in front of an international television audience. His 27.2-kilogram fleece was auctioned for charity — an average Merino fleece weighs around 4.5 kilograms. Later, Shrek was shorn on an iceberg floating 90 kilometres off the coast of Dunedin. In November 2008 the celebrity sheep was flown from Queenstown to Auckland to be trimmed for a third time, also in the interests of charity.

Romney

The Romney Marsh breed of sheep, from southeast England, arrived in New Zealand in 1853. It soon became known simply as the Romney, and by the early 1960s it accounted for three-quarters of this country's 50 million sheep. It is still New Zealand's most common sheep, numbering about 27 million. It is known as a dual-purpose animal, being equally important for meat and wool production.

Shearing

By the late 1880s shearing had become big business in New Zealand. With the introduction of shearing machines, large woolsheds became common. The first shearing machines were powered by steam and petrol-fired generators and, later, by electricity. In 1994 Te Kuiti, in the Waitomo district, proclaimed itself 'Shearing Capital of the World' when it unveiled its 6-metre-high statue of a shearer in a black singlet. Shearing was a competitive sport in New Zealand from the early 1900s. National championships began in 1960.

From the 1950s until the 1970s the scene was dominated by Godfrey

Bowen, born in Hastings in 1922, who developed a more efficient style of shearing and broke several world records. Another famous shearer is David Fagan who won the national shearing competition for the first time in 1986. He went on to win the New Zealand Golden Shears Open Championship 15 times. He also won a large number of world and United Kingdom titles.

Wool

In the early 1870s wool became New Zealand's main export item in terms of earnings, and it is still vital to the nation's economy. New Zealand is now second only to Australia in terms of the export of all types of wool, and is the world's largest producer and exporter of crossbred wool — wool that is produced by crossing fine- and long-wool sheep.

While most of New Zealand's wool has been exported, beginning in the last quarter of the nineteenth century it was also processed locally. The Mosgiel Woollen Mill, near Dunedin, was established in 1871 and was this country's first proper woollen mill. The Kaiapoi Woollen Manufacturing Company, in Canterbury, was established in 1878; by the end of the century it claimed to be first in the country to be lit by electricity and also the largest manufacturer in Australasia.

Woolshed

The largest and most important outbuilding on a sheep farm is the woolshed, where the sheep are shorn and the wool is sorted and packed. A typical woolshed has corrugated-iron cladding that is painted a dark red colour. The writer Samuel Butler, who lived as a sheepfarmer in Canterbury, from 1860 to 1864, wrote in his 1872 novel *Erewhon*: 'A wool shed is a roomy place, built somewhat on the same plan as a cathedral, with aisles on either side full of pens for the sheep, a great nave, at the upper end of which the shearers work, and a further space for wool sorters and packers.'

Wool press

In the early days workers simply trampled the wool clip into bales, but the job was made much easier with the development of mechanical presses. The tightly packed bales were then ready to be taken for sale at the woolstore.

Aerial topdressing

Spreading fertiliser on New Zealand farmland from the air really began in 1949, although there is a possibility that aircraft were used for topdressing as early as 1926. The idea caught on quickly in the 1950s, beginning with the use of twin-engined Tiger Moth aircraft to spread soil-enriching superphosphate and minerals. By 1966 there were about 10,000 airstrips dotted across the farms of New Zealand.

In recent times the main aircraft used for aerial topdressing in New Zealand has been the Fletcher FU24. Beginning in 1955, the Fletcher was developed in the United States for New Zealand conditions. Production shifted to Hamilton, New Zealand, and there are now about a hundred of them operating here.

Airtruck

The most unusual aircraft yet seen in New Zealand was a classic example of Kiwi ingenuity. The Airtruck, designed for aerial topdressing in 1960 to replace the Tiger Moth, was developed by Bennett Aviation of Te Kuiti, and later taken over by Waitomo Aviation Ltd. It was largely made from parts of surplus American Harvard aircraft bought from the Royal New Zealand Air Force. The cockpit was directly above a hopper that could carry 1.5 tonnes of fertiliser and this gave it its unusual appearance. Another unusual feature was the twin tail-booms, which may have been inspired by the RNZAF's Vampire fighter. Fertiliser trucks were able to back between these two booms to load the hopper and the pilot could take off without waiting for the truck to move off. Only two Airtrucks were built and both were destroyed in crashes.

Superphosphate

Superphosphate — known as super for short — was used from the early 1920s to provide New Zealand's pastures with essential phosphate, which was found to be lacking in New Zealand soils. This country's main supply of phosphate was the Pacific island of Nauru, where large deposits had formed from the droppings of local birds as a result of their fish-rich diet.

Grass

New Zealand's farming industry is based on grass and that makes grass our most important crop. Prior to the arrival of Europeans, only a small part of the country — mostly in the South Island — was covered by tussock-like native grasses. European settlers quickly set about removing tussock and bush cover, and planting their own imported grasses.

Burning off

Using fire to clear large areas of New Zealand bush to make way for farmland was common practice in early New Zealand. It was known as burning off or 'having a burn off'. Later, the area was known as a bush-burn. A farmer might identify an area of his farm which had recently been cleared and sowed with grass seed as 'the bush-burn'.

Gorse

Gorse was brought to New Zealand for use as a hedge, and soon grew out of control. As a result, in 1950 it was declared a noxious weed, along with 86 other 'troublesome' plants, including blackberry, boxthorn, foxglove, lupin and ragwort. All but two of these plants — two varieties of tauhinu or New Zealand cotton wood — had been introduced to this country.

Macrocarpa

A common tree in New Zealand, introduced from California, macrocarpa was originally planted to farm hedges and shelterbelts. The timber is similar to kauri.

Number-eight wire

The standard wire used for fencing on New Zealand farms is sold as eight-gauge wire — the gauge is the thickness of the wire. It is commonly known as number-eight wire. Because it has proved useful for many other purposes, such as handles for buckets made out of discarded kerosene tins, number-eight wire has come to represent Kiwi ingenuity — some people say Kiwis can fix anything with a piece of number-eight wire.

Strainers

Strainers — also known as a straining-posts or strainer posts — are an important part of a typical wire-and-batten farm fence. They are large posts included in the fence at regular distances and rammed into the ground to take the strain and keep the wires taut.

Taranaki gate

A fine example of Kiwi ingenuity and rural inventiveness, the Taranaki gate first appeared in the 1930s. It is made of wire — either number-eight or barbed wire — stapled to battens and strung between two strainers. It is attached to the strainers at both ends by loops of wire. They are cheap to make — no timber, hinges or catches required. Taranaki gates are very adaptable, suitable for use on sloping ground, and can be made on the spot to the length required. They are also easily repaired.

Electric fences

In the 1930s Hamilton farmer Bill Gallagher solved the problem of his horse, Joe, scratching himself on the family car by attaching an electrical device to the vehicle. In the late 1930s Gallagher developed the idea further into a business — Gallagher Power Fencing. Initially, the farm fences were powered by batteries. In the early 1960s Gallagher developed a low-cost mains-system electric fence that would be cheaper and more portable than standard fencing. The idea was a world leader, and the company developed markets in Australia and Europe.

Today the Hamilton-based Gallagher Group supplies its animal-control and agricultural fencing systems to more than 100 countries, where it is utilised by farms, wildlife parks, and conservation and protection programmes for plants and animals.

Saleyard

The saleyard, a large area of small pens for holding livestock for sale, was once an important part of most New Zealand towns in rural areas. The day when animals were sold by auction was known as sale day, and was the equivalent of a market day in English towns.

Paddock

Since the 1840s the word paddock has been used in New Zealand to describe an area of farmland enclosed either by a fence or some form of natural boundary. In 1842 a visitor to missionary John Morgan's property at Te Awamutu described: 'a garden stocked with young fruit-trees of every description . . . and a capital paddock laid down in English grasses.'

— *New Zealand Colonist and Port Nicholson Advertiser*, 19 August 1842

Stock and station agent

The stock and/or station agent was an important part of the rural community in New Zealand, and Australia, from the 1840s. The agent was attached to a large firm, and arranged the buying and selling of a farmer's stock. An agent would also give general advice on farming.

Federated Farmers

The first organisation to look after the interests of New Zealand farmers was formed in Kaitaia in 1899. This led to the formation of the nationwide New Zealand Farmers' Union in 1902. In 1945 the New Zealand Farmers' Union joined with the Sheepowners' Federation to form Federated Farmers of New Zealand. Today the organisation represents over 25,000 farming folk throughout New Zealand.

Apples

Apples (and pears) were introduced into New Zealand in 1819 by the Reverend Samuel Marsden, and by 1835 such trees were reported to be flourishing in the Bay of Islands. A trial shipment of apples was taken to Britain in cool storage in 1899, and encouraged an export trade which expanded in the years after the First World War.

Further to the main varieties — Gravenstein, Cox's Orange, Pippin, Golden Delicious, Jonathan, Sturmer and Granny Smith — in 1950 a new type of apple was discovered growing in an orchard in the Braeburn Valley, Nelson, and named the Braeburn. It is possible that it was, in part, derived from the popular apple variety known as the Granny Smith. The Braeburn is now one of the major apples

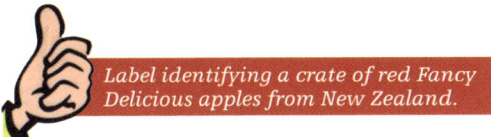

Label identifying a crate of red Fancy Delicious apples from New Zealand.

Cow COCKIES 219

produced in New Zealand and is grown throughout the world. In 1997 ENZA — formerly the New Zealand Apple and Pear Marketing Board — introduced the new Pacific Rose apple, which had been bred from the Cox's Orange Pippin and the Delicious.

Kiwifruit

About 1914 a Chinese fruit — originally called monkey peach — became available in New Zealand, where it was known as the Chinese gooseberry. When Auckland fruit and vegetable wholesaling company Turners and Growers planned to export the fruit to the United States the name was a problem. For a start, this Chinese gooseberry did not look like other gooseberries. As a result, in 1959, the decision was made to give the small, hairy brown fruit another name. They settled on the name kiwifruit and a very successful export enterprise took off as it quickly became accepted around the world.

Zespri

By the 1980s kiwifruit had become New Zealand's leading horticultural export. Unfortunately, the name kiwifruit had not been registered as a trademark and, so, other countries were able to use the name to market their own fruit. As a result, in 1996 the New Zealand kiwifruit industry decided it needed a brand name for its now world-famous product. They wanted an easily remembered name that reflected the essence of the fruit. They settled on the name Zespri — the word was computer-generated and does not stand for anything, but it soon came to be associated with kiwifruit from New Zealand. The New Zealand Kiwifruit Marketing Board now became Zespri International Ltd.

One of New Zealand's leading horticultural exports, the Kiwifruit, on a 1983 postage stamp.

Cow COCKIES 221

In 1999 Zespri launched its newly developed yellow-fleshed Zespri™ Gold variety to the world and its original green-fleshed kiwifruit was rebranded Zespri™ Green.

Tobacco

Tobacco came to New Zealand with the first European visitors. New Zealand proved suitable for growing the tobacco plant, but not all the local leaves ended up in pipes or cigarettes. Nicotine, a poisonous substance found in tobacco, was also found to be effective against pests around the farm — during the 1930s sheep were drenched against lice, ticks and scab with a tobacco-based drench that had a high nicotine sulphate content. The same product was also handy in the garden and chook run.

Forestry

Early European immigrants to New Zealand referred to native trees as pines, such as the kauri pine, black pine or miro, red pine or rimu, and white pine or kahikatea. Nowadays the name refers simply to the radiata pine, a Californian conifer which grows particularly well in New Zealand. Large-scale planting of these trees began in the early 1920s, in particular at the Kaingaroa Forest on the North Island's Volcanic Plateau.

Bees and honey

Bees play a vital part in the New Zealand economy, for as well as producing honey they pollinate a number of crops, including vegetables, fruit, and clover pastures for the dairy industry. New

Zealand has a small number of native bees, which do not live in hives, and the first honey bees were introduced in 1839.

White clover is the most common source of New Zealand honey, which is an important export. The varroa bee mite, which first appeared in New Zealand around 2000 and is now distributed throughout the North Island and as far south as Canterbury, is reducing the numbers of bees in both managed hives and wild colonies. This could have a disastrous impact on crop pollination, approximately one-third of the food New Zealanders eat relies on honey bees for pollination.

New Zealand bees also produce manuka honey, known for its anti-bacterial properties, while bee pollen is believed to boost immune function and detoxify the body.

Possums

Possums are a major pest in New Zealand, first introduced from Australia in 1858. Until 1947 the animal was protected, but since then it has become widespread throughout the country, ravaging native bush. As possums spread bovine tuberculosis they pose a threat to the dairy and meat industries. In 2000 the estimated number was a staggering 70 million possums, capable of munching their way through 20,000 tonnes of foliage every night. In recent years possum-fur clothing has become increasingly popular. Very warm and soft, it has the added bonus of being more politically correct to wear than other animal furs, as the animals cause such widespread damage.

Proud owners parade their pet calves in front of the judges at the Egmont A&P Show, Hawera, in south Taranaki.

Rabbits

Rabbits are another of New Zealand's greatest pests, first introduced in the late 1830s. Thirty years later they were well established in Otago and Southland, from where they moved north, destroying grasslands throughout the South Island. By the early 1960s there were 161 rabbit boards around New Zealand to deal with the problem.

In 1997, while the New Zealand government was considering the matter, the rabbit calicivirus (RCD) was illegally introduced to the country in an attempt to control the pest. Officially this was viewed as a breach of New Zealand's biosecurity, posing potential risk to ecosystems and other species.

A&P and A&H shows

Agricultural and pastoral or horticultural events have long been a feature of New Zealand's farming communities. The most popular have always been the annual A&P and A&H shows that feature a range of exhibits and competitions, such as dog trials, equestrian events, woodchopping, fencing, Highland dancing, cake baking, chutney making, photography and children's art competitions, along with the judging of farm animals. More recently, shows have included wild-food stalls, chainsaw sculpture and lawn-mower polo.

Fieldays

Now the largest agricultural show in the Southern Hemisphere, Fieldays began at the Te Rapa racecourse in 1969. The first event attracted about 15,000 people. The event moved to Mystery Creek in the Waikato in 1971, and in 2008 received nearly 132,000 visitors over four days. It now covers 240 hectares of exhibitions and attracts visitors from nearly 40 countries. It also draws international buyers and delegations, and the theme for the 2008 event was 'The Science of Farming'.

Backblocks and wop-wops

In the early days of settlement, a remote area of farmland was known as a back block. This led to the word backblocks, which now refers to thinly populated inland areas some distance from towns or cities. Inland areas, for example near the Southern Alps in Canterbury, are also referred to as the back country.

The Australian expression woop-woops — referring to a remote or distant area — has evolved in New Zealand as the wop-wops or, more simply, the wops. Similar to the backblocks, it's an area in an unpopulated area in the middle of nowhere.

Station

Long before it had any association with railway transport, a station in New Zealand was a place where a church mission or a farm had been established. By the mid-1800s a station could also refer to the homestead, and other buildings, associated with a large sheepfarming property. For example, in 1840 a Wellington newspaper advertised a forthcoming auction of farm animals to be held at 'Mr Watt's cattle and sheep station at Evan's Bay, at the west end of the harbour'.

— *New Zealand Gazette and Wellington Spectator*, 18 April 1840

She'll be right

The expression 'she'll be right' reflects an easy-going, relaxed Kiwi attitude that things will turn out for the best. Although the expression uses 'she', there is not necessarily anything feminine about the subject or situation being discussed. In 1955 New Zealander Peter Cape wrote a song which used the expression as its title and explained that the best attitude towards life's many problems is, predictably, 'Don't worry, mate, she'll be right'.

Cow cocky

The term cow cocky probably crossed the Tasman from Australia, and initially referred to a small-scale dairy farmer. New Zealand cow cockies are most likely to be found on the middle of the North Island, in Taranaki and Waikato.

Run

In the mid-nineteenth century, the idea of being able to 'run' sheep or cattle led to the use of 'run' for an area of land suitable for farming, particularly in Canterbury. Farmers took on such runs by lease or licence, and the land was owned by either the Crown or a local authority. Such a farmer was known as a run-holder — similar to the Australian squatter.

In 1855 new regulations increased the security of Canterbury run-holders. Any improvements made on the leased land, such as house and buildings, could not be bought from under the farmer.

Bugger

The word has been used in New Zealand since at least the 1860s, but it was not likely to be heard in polite circles until 1999 when a television advertisement that featured the word took the country by storm. The award-winning advertisement consisted of a series of humorous rural accidents, to which a farmer could only respond with one word — Bugger! The final scene shows his loyal dog, face down in the mud, muttering the same word.

Dag

A dag is a piece of wool clotted with dung that hangs around the hindquarters of a sheep. Because they attract blowflies, dags need to be removed. The dirty back end of a sheep has also inspired a number of expressions. For example, if someone tells you to 'rattle your dags' you need to hurry up. A 'bit of a dag' is a term used to describe something or someone amusing.

Queen Street farmer

The term Queen Street farmer first appeared in the deregulated economic climate of the 1980s, when city dwellers invested in rural activities for tax-deduction purposes. These people didn't work or live on their land at all. Popular investments for Queen Street farmers were deer-farming, forestry and the cultivation of kiwifruit.

Hard Yakker

Gumdigger

In the early twentieth century, kauri gum was a major New Zealand export, dug from the ground by gumdiggers in Northland. The gumdigger, with his spade and long, probing gum-spear, was peculiar to New Zealand, but disappeared when synthetic materials began to replace kauri gum in the manufacture of paints, polishes and floor coverings.

Dairy factories

In the late nineteenth century New Zealand was described as 'the Denmark of the South' on account of the growing importance of its dairy industry. The production of butter and cheese had begun on farms, and later led to the establishment of factories. The first was built at Edendale, Southland, in 1882. It had a herd of 300 cows and later used the services of a butter-maker brought from Denmark.

With the introduction of refrigerated shipping, dairy products became major exports, and by 1894 there were 62 butter factories, 55 cheese factories and 60 creameries around New Zealand, relying on milk provided by nearly 57,000 cows. At that time nearly one-third of all cheese factories were found in Southland, while Taranaki was home to over one-third of all butter factories.

By the late nineteenth century New Zealand's dairy factories had begun to amalgamate and form co-operatives. In 2001 there were 15 companies operating around 30 dairy factories, and five years later saw the formation of the giant cooperative Fonterra.

Anchor brand

One of New Zealand's oldest and best known international brand names began on a Waikato dairy farm, and is said to have been inspired by a former sailor's tattoo. When refrigerated shipping started, Henry Reynolds, a farmer, built the first butter factory in the Waikato at Pukekura, near Cambridge. In November 1886 Reynolds decided to give the first batch of butter the brand name Anchor. The business grew to include butter factories and creameries in Waikato, Bay of Plenty and Taranaki, producing butter that was sent to Australia, China, Hong Kong and England. In 1919, when a number of dairy companies were combined, the Anchor brand became the trademark of the New Zealand Co-operative Dairy Company.

Now over 120 years old, the Anchor trademark is owned by Fonterra and covers a wide range of products, including ready-to-drink and powdered milk, yoghurt, cheese and butter. Overseas it is available in Australia, the Philippines, Middle East, Pacific and United Kingdom.

Freezing works

In 1882 the ship *Dunedin* took the first cargo of refrigerated meat from New Zealand to Britain. This opened up a huge new market for this country, and within nine years there were 17 freezing works around the country providing carcasses for export. These were New Zealand's first large-scale industrial plants. From 1980 changes to the meat industry, such as technological advancements, resulted in the closure of some of the older works and the establishment of smaller facilities. The people who work there are known as freezing workers.

Hard YAKKER

Dairies

Around the late 1930s small stores selling groceries, including milk, butter and ice-cream, began to be known as dairies. Formerly known as corner stores, they were now referred to as corner dairies or simply dairies. The owners usually lived out the back or above the shop. In the 1960s when New Zealanders started driving to supermarkets for their weekly shopping, many dairies closed their doors. The small stores that have survived are open longer hours and their stock reflects the needs of the local neighbourhood.

Milkbars

In 1935 two business partners opened a new type of shop in Manners Street, Wellington — they sold only ice creams and milkshakes. They named it Tip Top (see page 243) and it was the first of many milkbars to open in the main streets of towns and cities nationwide. Later, milkbars also sold soft drinks, confectionery and light snacks and many provided booth seating for their customers. In the early 1950s milkbars became gathering places for motorcycle-riding youths who parked their bikes outside — they were called milkbar cowboys.h

Supermarkets

The supermarket was introduced to New Zealand by Tom Ah Chee, the son of a Chinese fruit-shop proprietor from south Auckland. He and two business partners bought a site in Otahuhu and the doors of their American-style supermarket — called Foodtown — opened on 18 June 1958. It was an instant success, and a second Foodtown was opened in Takanini, South Auckland in 1961. The way we buy our groceries was changed as the trend spread nationwide. New Zealand currently has six major supermarket chains owned by two grocery organisations — New World, Pak'nSave and Four Square owned by Foodstuffs, and Foodtown, Woolworths and Countdown by Progressive Entorprises

Woolworths

Woolworths is a big name in supermarkets in New Zealand, and began as a chain of variety stores. Australia had its first Woolworths when a bargain-basement store opened in Sydney in 1924. Five years later a company was formed to bring Woolworths to New Zealand. The stores were soon found in all the main cities and were affectionately known as Woollies.

McKenzies

McKenzies stores, which also came from Australia, were in competition with the original Woolworths variety stores. Their founder, John McKenzie, had a successful fancy-goods business in Melbourne, and opened his first New Zealand store in Dunedin in 1910. The McKenzie chain proved successful, and grew to 75 general merchandise stores. But in 1980 the business was merged with Woolworths, and the McKenzie name disappeared. Soon after, Woolworths stores became supermarkets and there are now 60 of these in New Zealand, as well as another 22 stores operating under the well-known name.

Feltex

In 1941 an footwear factory in Wellington became Felt and Textiles of New Zealand Ltd and began to make other products, including woollen felt and woven carpets, utilising New Zealand wool. Woollen felt was made from greasy wool, and pounded in a milling machine to produce the once well-known floor coverings, which have carpeted the floors of many New Zealand houses. The company became known as Feltex, but in 2006 it went into receivership and was bought by Australia's leading carpet company.

Bookshops

New Zealand is said to have more bookstores per head of population than any other country and, according to the findings of a 2002 survey, buying books is our most popular cultural activity.

In recent years the three top-selling New Zealand books of all time have been: Alison Holst's *Marvellous Muffins*, 1994, Michael King's *Penguin History of New Zealand*, 2003, and Lynley Dodd's *Hairy Maclary from Donaldson's Dairy*, 1983.

Whitcoulls

Whitcoulls, a major New Zealand chain of bookstores, was formed in 1971 with the merger of two well-established companies, Whitcombe & Tombs and Coulls Somerville Wilkie. Bookseller George Whitcombe formed a partnership with printer George Tombs in 1882 and opened a shop in Cashel Street, Christchurch. Formed in 1871, Coulls

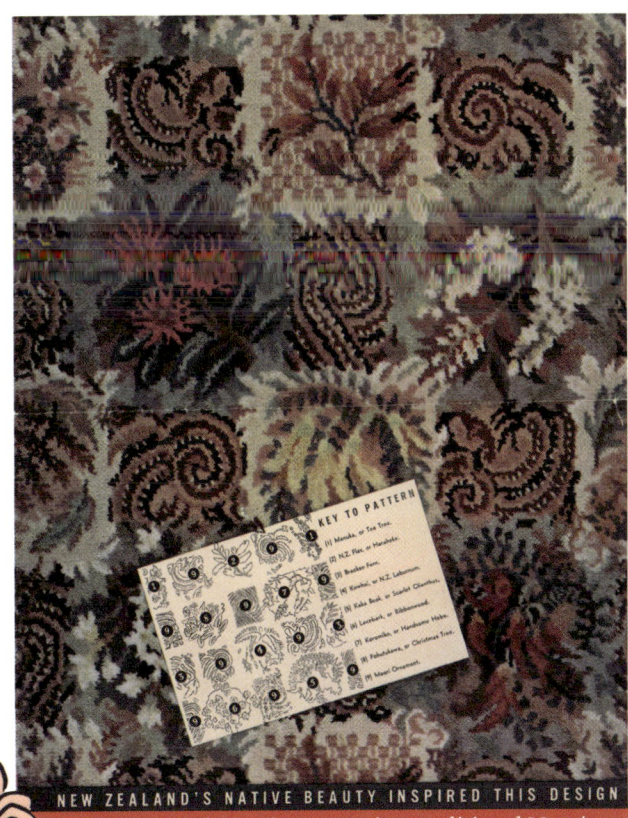

NEW ZEALAND'S NATIVE BEAUTY INSPIRED THIS DESIGN

A woven carpet design incorporating traditional Maori motifs manufactured by Felt and Textiles New Zealand Ltd, a company better known as Feltex.

Hard YAKKER

Somerville Wilkie was a major printing company based in Dunedin. The Whitcoulls chain now has 65 stores nationwide — 40 of which are in Auckland, Wellington and Christchurch.

Publishing

In 1842 the first book was printed in New Zealand — the subject was Maori grammar. Then, for most of the twentieth century, New Zealand's leading book publishers were A.H. & A.W. Reed, which originated in Dunedin in 1907, and Whitcombe and Tombs. Up until 1990, the country's best-selling books in multiple editions were: *Edmonds Cookery Book* with a total of more than 3.45 million copies sold, and *Yates Gardening Guide*, with more than one million copies sold.

Four Square

In the 1920s, facing competition from chain stores, a group of New Zealand grocers got together to form a co-operative. The name for their company was born when the secretary doodled on his calendar and drew a square around the date — 4 July 1924. It just happened to be American Independence Day, so perhaps it was a fitting symbol of independence (from the chain stores) for the private grocer in New Zealand. The symbol was adopted, and the Four Square group grew to have 112 member stores by 1931 and 700 by 1950. Around 1947 it acquired its other well-known symbol — the smiling grocer in an apron with a pencil behind his ear that was based on an actual grocer, George Allan. That grocer has since gained another life outside the store in the hands of artist Dick Frizzell.

The familiar smiling grocer who began attending to Four Square customers in the late 1940s.

Department stores

Department stores first appeared in Europe and the United States from the 1830s and arrived in New Zealand in the 1860s. The earliest department stores were Beaths and Ballantynes in Christchurch; Brown, Ewing & Co and the Draper Importing Company (DIC) in Dunedin; Kirkcaldie and Stains in Wellington; and George Court and Smith & Caughey in Auckland. In recent years many of those names have been lost as companies have merged and been renamed or as department stores have given way to shopping malls.

Farmers Trading Company

New Zealand's largest department store started trading in 1909 as a mail-order business. Robert Laidlaw produced his first catalogue, containing a large range of items — from crockery to saddles — for the nation's homes and farms. He then moved to retailing, with a store in Auckland's Hobson Street. In 1922 it was the first department store in the country to provide a free bus service for customers — the buses ran from Queen Street to Hobson Street. Other firsts were a rooftop children's playground that opened in 1922, escalators that were installed in 1955 and a shoppers' car park, which was provided in 1957. The Farmers company continues to operate 55 department stores around the country. Another Farmers tradition that has survived is the Santa Parade, which has been held in Auckland and Christchurch since 1947.

Shopping malls

New Zealand was introduced to a new shopping experience in 1963 with the opening of the first mall — LynnMall, in West Auckland. This pioneering mall offered Kiwis the chance for the first time to do all their shopping under one roof. It was also the first in the country to be air-conditioned (in 1987), to introduce Sunday trading (in 1991), and to become smoke-free (in 1994). Today almost every town in New Zealand has a mall while the main centres have multiple malls.

Opening hours

For most of the twentieth century, New Zealand was closed over the weekend. But shopping hours began to change in the early 1980s. From 1990 retailers were able to choose their own opening hours. There were now only three and a half days when most shops were required to be closed — Christmas Day, Good Friday and Easter Sunday for the whole day, and until 1pm on ANZAC Day. Some shops were allowed to be open for business on those days, subject to certain conditions. For example, dairies and service stations could only sell essential goods, such as baby- and- pet foods; other shops could sell services, such as cutting hair, but not goods.

Late-night shopping

Until the 1980s, shops were open late one night of the week — until 9.00 pm instead of 5.30 pm. In most places this was on a Friday night and late-night shopping was a last chance to stock up on things for the weekend ahead. Prior to 1960, people would dress up for the occasion and for many, before television arrived, it was an important social activity.

Wattie's

In 1934 James Wattie began a fruit pulping and canning business in Hastings, and within two years the company was processing 25,000 cans per day — mostly pears and peaches. In 1946 the company produced its first frozen foods, an idea that had recently been developed in the United States. A new Wattie's factory opened in Gisborne in 1951. New Zealand's cats and dogs were catered for with the launch of Felix and Fido petfoods in 1955, and later Chef Jellimeat came onto the market in 1969. Wattie Industries Ltd, established in 1971, became the largest food-processing group in New Zealand.

The company employs around 1900 people at its three production centres in New Zealand, two in Hastings — one of which is on the site of the original factory — and one in Christchurch.

Hallensteins

In 1884 German-born Bendix Hallenstein and his two brothers established the first Drapery Importing Company — a department store called DIC, in Dunedin. They also set up the country's first clothing factory and warehouse in response to a difficulty in sourcing quality menswear from overseas, and Hallenstein Bros. stores selling menswear. In 1985 Hallensteins merged with womenswear chain Glassons. Both facets of the business remain market leaders today.

Wattie's peas were the inspiration for this float in the once annual Hastings Blossom Festival.

Hard YAKKER 241

Sanitarium

In 1898 Sanitarium — the name behind a number of well-known New Zealand brands — began importing products from the United States. In 1900 the company built a small wooden shed in Papanui, Christchurch, where it began making Granola, Caramel Cereal and bread. In 1919 it also began selling Marmite (see page 37), which, at first, it imported from England. The company is still in Papanui today. Sanitarium added Weet-Bix (see page 34) to its range in 1930.

Glaxo

At the beginning of the twentieth century Joseph Nathan and Sons quickly realised the potential for the export of dried milk powder. The company obtained the Australian and New Zealand patent for this product. In May 1904 John Merrett, an English engineer employed by Nathans, produced the first dried milk processed in New Zealand at the Nathans' Makino factory. Marketing their new product as a baby food, they called it Glaxo. By the end of that year they had a new purpose-built dried-milk processing factory in Bunnythorpe that continued to produce dried milk for the next 70 years.

From 1937 Glaxo began to manufacture pharmaceuticals, and in 1973 the company moved to Palmerston North, where it operated until 1996. It later became part of the international pharmaceutical company GlaxoSmithKline.

Tip Top

The biggest name in ice cream in New Zealand had its origins in the mid-1930s when Albert Hayman and Len Malaghan opened the country's first milkbar in Manners Street, Wellington. They called it Tip Top after hearing a fellow diner in a restaurant say his meal was 'tip top'. The Tip Top Ice Cream Company went into business in 1936, and two years later was manufacturing its own ice cream and operating stores in the lower half of the North Island, Nelson and Blenheim.

In 1938 Tip Top opened a factory in Auckland. The ice cream business continued to grow, and a parent company, General Foods Corporation (NZ) Ltd was formed in 1964. In 2001 Tip Top Ice Cream became part of Fonterra — now New Zealand's biggest company. Today Tip Top produces 50 million litres of ice cream per year in different forms, including the brands Trumpet, FruJu, Jelly Tip, and Memphis Meltdown. Many New Zealanders well remember the Trumpet ads of the 1980s that featured a young Rachel Hunter in her screen debut. She went on to become an international supermodel.

Fisher & Paykel

In 1934 Maurice Paykel and Woolf Fisher began one of New Zealand's most innovative companies, starting as an importer of electrical home appliances. But in 1939 the government placed restrictions on such goods and Fisher & Paykel had no choice but to become manufacturers. They started with wringer washing machines and refrigerators, and in 1956 began making a rotary clothes-drier of their own design. Fisher & Paykel entered the healthcare market in 1971 with the development of a respiratory humidifier system for use in critical care. The advanced SmartDrive autowasher was launched in 1991, followed by the award-winning DishDrawer in 1997, by which time F&P was the biggest whiteware manufacturer in Australasia.

Crown Lynn

In 1940 Auckland's Amalgamated Brick and Pipe Company began making crockery, and one of its first orders was a handleless mug for use in the New Zealand Railways refreshment tearooms. Around 1943 this item was given a handle, and became the well-known, extremely durable and chunky Railways cup. This department of the company, located in Auckland's New Lynn, became known as Crown Lynn. It produced domestic crockery and decorative items, including a range of animal figures — the best known are the kiwi and swan vases. Crown Lynn passed a milestone in 1959 when it produced its 100 millionth piece of pottery, but the company was unable to compete with cheaper imported goods and closed in 1989.

Bottle store and shop

In New Zealand the part of a hotel that sells alcohol for drinking elsewhere is usually known as a bottle store. Alcohol is also sold retail by wine and spirit merchants. These days, too, there are stores that specialise only in wine.

Shouting

In New Zealand and Australia the practice of paying for someone else's drink in a public bar is known as shouting. It is presumed the expression came about because the customer had to shout to be heard above the general noise in the bar. When people drink in a group, a drinking session might involve each member buying a round of drinks for the group — this became known as 'shouting a round'. During the First World War, regulations aimed at reducing consumption of alcohol made the practice of shouting or paying for a round of drinks illegal.

Six o'clock swill

In 1917, as a wartime measure, regulations required New Zealand's hotel bars to close at 6.00 pm. This led to what became known in this country as the six o'clock swill. Drinkers who finished work at 5.00 pm had, at most, an hour's drinking time. Six o'clock closing lasted nearly 50 years and was finally changed in October 1967 when hotel bars could remain open until 10.00 pm.

The weekend

For much of the twentieth century New Zealand was noted for its slow weekends, when very little was open for business. This dated back to 1894, when laws were passed to stop shops trading from midday on Saturday until Monday morning. The general attitude was, therefore, that New Zealanders worked five days a week for someone else but the weekend was for enjoying themselves with their families or, perhaps, working at home in the garden or shed. The weekend changed when Saturday shopping was introduced in 1980 and, by the end of the decade, shopping hours were extended further to include Sunday.

Mate's rates

In Australia and New Zealand, mate's rates are reduced charges (for goods and services) that are usually reserved for friends and acquaintances.

The term mate can apply not only to a close friend but also to another individual who may not necessarily be a friend. Thus, 'Just a minute, mate', might be said in an attempt to gain a stranger's attention. An old mate is certainly a friend.

The works

To give something or someone the works means that nothing is held back, e.g. 'I'd like the works on my burger, please.' The works also refers to a factory where physical work is carried out, or to the freezing works — animals are sent to the works to be slaughtered.

Yakker

Yakker, also spelled yakka and yacker, means work. The word came to New Zealand from Australia in the late nineteenth century. Nowadays it is mostly used in the context of hard yacker, which means particularly strenuous work. In 1898 an Otago newspaper published a lengthy poem, 'The Song of a Rolling Stone', in which the poet, in search of work, was told by his old mate to go to Southland, where: 'You'll be sure to get some yacker, and more country you will see'.

— *Otago Witness*, 31 March 1898

Pedal to the METAL

Filling up, circa 1960, at a Caltex service station in the Hutt Valley.

State Highway 1

State Highway 1, or simply SH1, is New Zealand's main road. Currently 2047 kilometres long, it runs the length of both main islands from its northernmost point at Cape Reinga to Bluff at the bottom of the South Island. Just before reaching Ashburton, in Canterbury, the highway crosses the country's longest road bridge over the Rakaia River. Because of regular straightening to remove dangerous bends, State Highway 1 keeps getting shorter — in 1950 the distance by road between Auckland and Wellington was 660 kilometres, but by 1999 it had been reduced by 11 kilometres.

The Desert Road

Where State Highway 1 crosses part of the the Volcanic Plateau between Turangi (near the south end of Lake Taupo) and Waiouru is known as the Desert Road. The name comes from the sandy wasteland to the west of the road, known as the Rangipo Desert. The Desert Road reaches 1074 metres above sea level, which is the highest point in the New Zealand state highway system. The route provides spectacular views of three volcanoes — Mount Tongariro, Mount Ngauruhoe and Mount Ruapehu. It is frequently closed by snow during winter.

Cars

New Zealand's first petrol-driven car appeared in Wellington in 1898. In 1909 the world's most famous automobile, the Model T Ford, arrived and it proved to be ideal for local conditions. By the early 1930s nearly 80 per cent of all new cars sold in this country were American. This dominance was broken by the British Vauxhall, whose 26hp VX model appeared in 1931 and was claimed to be 'the first English car built for New Zealand roads'. By 1975, when the New Zealand motorist was facing rising fuel costs, the Ford Cortina was the country's best-selling car, but Hondas, Datsuns and Toyotas — in particular the Toyota Corolla — had just arrived. By the 1980s Japanese cars dominated the roads of New Zealand, and it has been that way ever since.

Ute

The ute, short for utility vehicle, is claimed as an Australian invention. The story goes that in 1933 a Gippsland farmer, who could not afford both a truck and a car, suggested to Ford Australia that they combine the two. They took him up on it and the first Ford ute was produced the following year. The idea of a vehicle with the comfort of a car and the utility of a truck soon spread worldwide.

The ute crossed the Tasman and proved popular in New Zealand, where it was celebrated in a series of hair-raising television advertisements for the Toyota Hi Lux starring Barry Crump.

Warrants of fitness

Since the 1930s New Zealand cars, including vans, utes and 4WDs, have been required to have a certificate of roadworthiness known as a warrant of fitness or WOF. Vehicles need to have inspections for warrants at approved garages and testing stations every 12 months, or every six months if the car was first registered over six years ago. It is illegal to drive a car which doesn't meet WOF requirements and does not display a valid WOF sticker in the top, driver's-side, inside corner of the front windscreen.

Remuera tractor

Nickname given to 4WD vehicles and SUVs (sport utility vehicles) which are used for mostly urban purposes in an upmarket Auckland suburb. The Melbourne equivalent is known as the Toorak tractor.

Trekka

In the 1960s, government import policies made new cars both expensive and hard to get in New Zealand. The Trekka was an Auckland company's attempt to produce an affordable local vehicle. It was based on the chassis and engine of a Skoda car imported from Czechoslovakia, with a New Zealand-made steel body and canvas or fibreglass canopy. The first Trekka appeared in 1964, and it was a steady seller. However, with the relaxation of import restrictions from 1970, it could not compete with Japanese vehicles and production ceased a few years later. About 2500 were produced but only a few dozen remain roadworthy.

In 2003 the vehicle was showcased in artist Michael Stevenson's installation *This is the Trekka*, New Zealand's contribution to the Venice Biennale.

Automobile Association

In 1898 New Zealand saw its first motor car and five years later a group of enthusiasts formed the Auckland Automobile Association. Motorists in the other main centres around New Zealand soon formed their own versions of the association, too. From the 1920s these bodies took responsibility for supplying road maps.

In 1965 the country's regional automobile associations merged to form the New Zealand Automobile Association, which claims to be the most popular club in the country.

Carless days

As the international oil crisis worsened in the late 1970s, the New Zealand government under Robert Muldoon introduced a number of measures to save fuel and costs. These included a 'carless days' scheme that came into effect on 30 July 1979 and required all owners of private motor vehicles to nominate one day of the week when their car would be off the road. Each car displayed a sticker which indicated the chosen day. The scheme did little to reduce New Zealand's consumption of petrol and carless days were quickly scrapped in May 1980.

Farm and quad bikes

New Zealand farmers once depended on the horse and, later, the tractor to get around their farms. Today they are more likely to be seen on a robust motorcycle known as a farm bike.

Another popular way of getting round farms in New Zealand now is on a four-wheeled all-terrain vehicle known as a quad bike. These vehicles are also known as ATVs — short for 'all-terrain vehicle'. Originally developed for recreational use in the 1980s, quad bikes now number an estimated 70,000 on New Zealand's farms.

Right-hand rule

In 1977 New Zealand drivers were required to follow a new rule that was designed to improve traffic flow at intersections. Drivers turning left now had to give way to right-turning traffic approaching in the opposite direction. The rule came from Victoria, Australia, where it was originally brought in to assist trams on inner-city Melbourne streets. But Victoria changed its rule in 1993 and New Zealand is now the only country in the world with a right-hand rule. A number of national organisations feel strongly that the rule should be changed, but it seems the government believes it would be confusing for the public.

Main trunk line

The main trunk line — also known as the main trunk railway — is the country's principal railway line. It runs between Auckland and Wellington and — like State Highway 1 — it continues between Picton and Invercargill.

Raurimu Spiral

The Raurimu Spiral is a world-famous engineering feat that enables the main trunk railway to climb and cross an area in the central North Island between Raurimu and National Park. The ascending spiral was designed in 1898, and includes a complete circle, three horseshoe curves and two tunnels.

The TranzAlpine train, with the Southern Alps as backdrop.

254 Crikey!

New Zealand Railways

New Zealand's first steam railway, between Christchurch and Ferrymead, was opened in late 1863. Sixteen years later the country's first trunk line — running between Christchurch and Invercargill — was completed. Work began on a central route for the North Island main trunk line in 1885. The country's rail system reached its greatest length — 5656 kilometres — in 1953. The last scheduled steam-train service ran on 26 October 1971.

Rail New Zealand now operates three long-distance services mainly for tourists: the Overlander between Auckland and Wellington; the TranzCoastal between Picton and Christchurch; and the TranzAlpine between Greymouth and Christchurch.

The Limited

The Limited Express — usually known simply as the Limited — was the express train that used to run on the main trunk line between Auckland and Wellington.

Railcar

In 1937 New Zealanders were able to travel by diesel-powered railcar for the first time when six 49-seater carriages were introduced, initially connecting Wellington and Palmerston North via Wairarapa. In 1955, 35 railcars seating 88 went into service on provincial routes around the country. They continued until they were withdrawn in 1978, leaving only the Silver Fern Express railcar running between Auckland and Wellington with a daily service in each direction.

Pedal to the METAL

Silver Fern railcar

The Silver Fern was the daylight railcar service on the main trunk line between Auckland and Wellington. It ran from December 1972 until December 1991, when it was replaced by the Overlander carriage train. The Silver Fern railcars were moved to other routes — between Auckland and Tauranga and Rotorua and Hamilton, but these services were unsuccessful and were stopped in October 2001. The railcars now run a commuter service between Auckland and Pukekohe.

Refrigerated shipping

In 1882 the sailing ship *Dunedin* successfully carried the first refrigerated cargo of New Zealand meat to England. This opened up a new era for this country's sheep farmers, who were able to supply the huge British market with mutton. Within nine years of the *Dunedin*'s voyage there were 17 freezing works established around New Zealand and by 1889 this country had exported over one million sheep carcasses.

Jet boat

In 1951 William Hamilton began to develop his ideas for a boat to explore shallow rivers. Propellers could not be used, and by 1956 he was achieving speeds of 80 kph in his new craft that used a water-jet propulsion system. Hamilton Jet Boats went into production soon after, and their boats have since navigated rivers around the world, from the Colorado to the Ganges.

Crikey!

Beaut

By the late nineteenth century the word 'beauty' was being used to describe something that was particularly special or delightful. In 1896 the Adams Star Cycle Company, of Christchurch advertised its ladies' bicycle as 'a little beauty'. Later, beauty became shortened to just beaut, and it is often qualified with a suitable adjective, as in 'bloody beaut' or 'real beaut'.

TEAL

Beginning in 1940, Tasman Empire Airways Ltd — TEAL — provided a flying-boat service between Sydney and Auckland. The 1200-mile trip took nine hours and in 1946 there were seven return flights a week. From 1950 to 1960 TEAL also ran flying-boat services between Auckland and Fiji, and from Fiji, services ran to Tonga, Western Samoa and the Cook Islands.

TEAL became fully owned by the New Zealand government in 1961 and entered the jet age in 1965 when it purchased three Douglas DC8 airliners. Later that year it changed its name to Air New Zealand.

NAC

In 1947 the New Zealand government nationalised and combined three smaller airlines to create the National Airlines Corporation, known as NAC. An important aircraft used by the new airline was the Douglas Dakota, or DC3. NAC grew to dominate domestic commercial air travel, servicing all provincial cities and larger towns until 1978 when it was taken over by Air New Zealand.

Passengers boarding a DC3 aircraft, the workhorse of the early NAC fleet.

Air New Zealand

In 1990 the national airline expanded operations by taking over Ansett Australia. However, increasing costs and international competition caused Ansett to cease operations in 2002.

Since 1973, the Air New Zealand symbol has been the Maori koru — a stylised representation of an unfolding fern frond (see page 264). Aircraft have also carried other decorations for special occasions, such as the image of All Black players on the aircraft that took the team to the 1999 Rugby World Cup and, in 2002 and 2003, imagery relating to *The Lord of the Rings* film trilogy.

Richard Pearse

Richard William Pearse was a born inventor. As a schoolboy in Canterbury he invented a needle threader for his mother and in 1902, aged 25, he received his first patent — for a new type of bicycle. By then he had built a workshop to pursue his interest in building a heavier-than-air machine that would fly. After much experimentation his aircraft took off, briefly, at Waitohi in South Canterbury. There is confusion over the date, and it may have been in March 1903. If so, it pre-dated the Wright Brothers' first flight in December 1903, but Pearse never claimed to be first — he believed his short hops in the air did not qualify as sustained flight. While he may not have been the first in the world to fly, he was the first British subject to manage a powered take-off in a heavier-than-air machine of his own design and construction. He died in 1953.

Go BUSH

Kauri

The New Zealand kauri is one of the world's largest trees. It is noted for its tall straight trunk free of branches. It was once an important source of timber, both for local construction and export. The tree also produces a resin or gum, which was collected by gumdiggers and sold for use in the production of paints, varnishes and polishes.

Kauri forest once covered much of the northern part of the North Island. Now, Waipoua in Northland is the last sizeable kauri forest. There visitors can see Tane Mahuta, God of the Forest — a kauri tree that stands 51.5 metres tall and is believed to be about 1200 years old.

Nikau

The nikau is a distinctive tree that grows throughout the North Island and in the top of the South Island, as far south as Greymouth and Banks Peninsula. It is the southernmost palm tree in the world. Nikau leaves were used as a roofing material by Maori, but in 1843 the use of nikau, raupo and similar such materials for building was outlawed in Wellington on account of the fire hazard.

Cabbage tree

One of New Zealand's most familiar trees, cabbage trees are known by the Maori as ti. The cabbage tree has a slender trunk up to 7.5 metres tall, and its head has a mass of broad leaves between 60 cm and one metre long. The trees are found throughout New Zealand, growing in swamps, beside rivers and on open plains. The Maori also traditionally used the long root of the tree as a source of food. However, in recent years large numbers of cabbage trees have died from a bacterium.

Pohutukawa

The pohutukawa tree's natural habitat is the coast as far south as New Plymouth and Gisborne. Because its bright-red flowers are on show at the end of the year it is known as the New Zealand Christmas tree. The oldest and largest pohutukawa tree is at Te Araroa, on the East Cape — it is nearly 20 metres tall and is believed to be over 600 years old. New Zealand's best-known pohutukawa grows at Cape Reinga, at the northern tip of the North Island and, according to Maori tradition, is the place from where spirits depart this world.

Flax

Flax — called harakeke by Maori — is a distinctive plant with long pointed leaves. It is found throughout New Zealand, especially in swampy land. Flax fibre was put to a wide range of uses by the Maori, including for clothing and fishing lines, and European settlers were quick to see its potential, too. In addition to rope, flax was also used to make wool packs for transporting the nation's wool clip.

One of the most iconic items of Maori art, which also has a practical use, is the flax-woven kete (basket). The kete was originally used for carrying food.

A magnificent flowering of pohutukawa blossom, justifying its claim as the 'New Zealand Christmas tree'.

Raupo

Raupo, the New Zealand bullrush, is a common swamp plant often found growing alongside flax. It was used as a building material by Maori and early European settlers. Maori also ate parts of the plant.

Biddy-bid

The biddy-bid — also known as biddy-biddy and bidi-bid — is a plant whose fruit has small hooks which can attach themselves to things — socks, in particular, and the wool of passing sheep. As a result it can be a nuisance for trampers and farmers. The name comes from the Maori piripiri.

Toetoe

The tall and graceful toetoe is New Zealand's largest native grass, growing in clumps up to three metres tall. It is found in a range of locations throughout the country and is closely related to pampas grasses that were introduced from South America for stock feed.

The Maori used the leaves and stalks of the toetoe for making baskets and mats and for tukutuku panelling. In 1855 a Wanganui land agent advertised 'several valuable sections consisting of river frontages, toetoe flats, bush sections, and undulating fern land'.

— *Taranaki Herald*, 14 February 1855

Koru

The unfurling frond of the fern is known as the koru. As a symbol of new life and growth the motif plays an important part in Maori art and design and has been adopted by Air New Zealand (see page 259). The koru has also been suggested to feature on a national flag, and was a regular element in the paintings of artist Gordon Walters.

Bush

Bush — an alternative New Zealand term for forest — was once the most predominant feature of the New Zealand landscape. For Kiwis, 'going bush' means either heading off on a camping, tramping or hunting trip or withdrawing from society. As the bush made way for farmland it also enriched the local language. For example, a bushworker or bushman might wear a bushman's singlet and a bush shirt.

Kiwi

The kiwi is an unofficial national symbol of New Zealand. It is a flightless nocturnal bird, with fur-like feathers, and nostrils near the top of its long tapered bill, which it pokes into the ground to search for worms and insects. It also eats fruit. The female kiwi lays an egg which is extremely large in relation to her body size. There are believed to be five species of kiwi; all are endangered as their numbers have been depleted by destruction of the bush and by introduced predators, such as possums, stoats, cats and dogs.

Moa

Large flightless birds called moa were once found throughout New Zealand. Early Maori hunted moa for food and the birds are believed to have become extinct before Europeans arrived here. In 1839 a small fragment of moa bone was taken to London and shown to leading scientist Sir Richard Owen. He announced to the scientific world that a bird that could have been as big as the ostrich had once lived in New Zealand. There are believed to have been about 10 different species of moa. The largest was the giant moa — one of the biggest birds ever known — and the smallest was about the size of a turkey.

Fantail

Known to many Maori as piwakawaka, the fantail is a lively and friendly insect-eating bird whose tail resembles a spread fan. It is found in the bush and domestic gardens and often enters houses chasing insects. In 1899 a Wellington newspaper described the fantail as: 'the fascinating little marquise of the Bush fancy dress ball . . . Flitting about the room, here, there, and everywhere . . . about the bush or on the surface of the water, throwing itself into every conceivable attitude, picturesque and fantastic, in its hunt after flies'.

— *Evening Post*, 4 February 1899

Huia

The huia, extinct since the early 1900s, was a forest bird found in the lower North Island. It was noted for its green and black plumage. Its white-tipped tail feathers were highly prized by Maori as symbols of rank — they were kept in ornately carved treasure boxes known as waka huia. In 1836 an explorer, Ernst Dieffenbach, described seeing four huia: 'After an extensive journey in the hilly forest in search of them, I had at last the pleasure of seeing four alight on the lower branches of the trees near which the native accompanying me stood. They came quick as lightning, descending from branch to branch, spreading out the tail and throwing up the wings.'

Godwit

Known to the Maori as kuaka, the godwit is a medium-sized wading bird that undertakes lengthy migratory flights from New Zealand to breeding grounds in Siberia and Alaska. A 1938 novel, *The Godwits Fly* by Robin Hyde, gave rise to the use of the word in relation to the lengthy journeys New Zealanders make — usually to England and Europe — in search of their cultural roots in England.

Kotuku

Known to Pakeha as the white heron, the kotuku is rare in New Zealand. The bird's only breeding ground in New Zealand is near Okarito, in Westland. The kotuku features in Maori legend representing rarity and beauty and it was selected as the symbol for New Zealand's 150th anniversary in 1990. Also, New Zealanders born that year received a birth certificate with an image of the rare bird.

Pukeko

The pukeko is a New Zealand swamp hen with a red bill and legs, black head and a purple and blue body. The bird doesn't fly, and has a distinctive way of walking and bobbing its head. It is found in lowland swamps and increasingly in urban areas, such as coastal land beside motorways. Due to this tendency to lurk on the edges of motorways, a large number of pukeko have met their ends on the roads in recent years. The birds also live in Australia as purple swamp-hens

Takahe

The takahe is a flightless bird which was known to be rare in the nineteenth century. From 1898 it was presumed extinct until Dr Geoffrey Orbell discovered a colony of about 12 pairs near Te Anau, in Fiordland, in 1948. The vividly coloured bird is now subject to an intense recovery plan, but it is still on the endangered list.

Tui

The tui is a member of a family of honey-eating birds found in Indonesia, Australia, New Zealand and parts of the Pacific. It lives in forest areas, parks and gardens throughout New Zealand. It has a white tuft at its throat and is also known as the parson bird. It is distinguished by a song that can vary according to location.

The bird has enjoyed a great deal of publicity in recent times due to a controversial advertising campaign by the beer company Tui. The Tui brewery originated in 1889, however it really came into the public eye in a big way with its advertising billboard series that featured a series of unlikely slogans followed by the words 'Yeah, right', which appealed to many New Zealanders' dry sense of humour. Here's an example: 'I love it when you talk during the rugby'. 'Yeah, right'.

Captain Cooker

The usual name for wild pigs in New Zealand is Captain Cooker. These animals were brought to this country by Captain Cook (see page 286) in 1773. He presented pigs that he had obtained from the Society Islands and Tonga to Maori near Cape Kidnappers in Hawke's Bay and at Queen Charlotte Sound. He later introduced more pigs to the country, as did European and American sealers and traders. These animals took to the New Zealand bush and were soon widespread throughout the country. Today pig hunters use dogs to corner and catch them for wild pork.

Pelorus Jack

Pelorus Jack was the name of a dolphin — probably a Risso's dolphin — that became well-known to ships passing through French Pass, to the north of Pelorus Sound, in the Marlborough Sounds. The friendly dolphin accompanied ships from 1888 until 1912. He received government protection in 1904.

Opo

During the summer of 1955–56 a young female bottle-nosed dolphin became a daily visitor at Opononi, in Hokianga Harbour. Named Opo, she would accompany boats and play with bathers at the beach. The government passed regulations that provided the same sort of protection given to Pelorus Jack in 1904, but in March 1956 the friendly dolphin died in mysterious circumstances. Opononi's famous visitor is honoured in the form of a statue by sculptor Russell Clark, and also by a catchy song written in 1956 by musician Crombie Murdoch.

Sandflies

In 1848 intrepid explorer Thomas Brunner went in search of a pass across the Southern Alps and encountered swarms of sandflies. He described how Maori lit fires to create smoke around the doorways to their houses to prevent the insects from going inside. Sandflies are among New Zealand's most annoying insects. They prefer to live on the edge of bush and the banks of lakes and on our beaches. The adult female is an aggressive blood-sucker, dining when it can on humans and other warm-blooded animals. It is not surprising that this small insect has given its name to some of New Zealand's geographical features, including Sandfly Bay — there's one on the south coast of the Otago Peninsula and one on the shores of Lake Wakatipu — and Sandfly Stream, inland from Kaikoura.

Glow worms

Glow worms are found throughout New Zealand but are best known for their display in the Waitomo Caves, in the King Country. The worms are larvae or grubs of a small fly. They have luminous tail portions that attract insects to the sticky fishing lines they hang from their bodies to catch their food.

Huhu

The huhu is the largest native beetle, and its grub or larva is found in decaying wood, which is its main food. In 1870 the ornithologist Walter Buller described a huhu grub the size of 'a man's little finger'. Huhu beetles are edible and have been described by some as tasting like buttery chicken. It's possible to partake in this culinary delight at Hokitika's Wild Food Festival, which has been operating since 1990.

Weta

The weta is the most spectacular New Zealand insect. There are several species of weta and they belong to the same family as grasshoppers, locusts and crickets. There are cave wetas with very long feelers and giant wetas that are among the heaviest insects in the world, but the best known is the tree weta that is often found in rotten logs, old tree trunks and garden hedges. The male has a large head and may appear fierce, but although it can bite it is otherwise harmless.

The weta has been made famous due to the adoption of its name by Wellington-based special effects company Weta Workshop (see page 123).

Two-toothed borer

There are several species of wood-boring beetles in New Zealand, and the largest is the native two-toothed longhorn borer. This insect has changed its habits, moving from the forest to wooden houses, where it can cause a large amount of damage. Borer like moist untreated timber and are often found on the south sides of buildings that are more likely to be damp, dark places. New Zealanders living in older houses, such as villas, may be familiar with the smaller species of borer that leave tell-tale holes and tracks on floorboards. It is commonly joked that it is only the borer holding hands that keep some of our older wooden houses from falling down.

Katipo

The katipo spider is found on beaches living under stones and driftwood and in sheltered plants. It is mostly black, and is distinguished by an orange stripe on its back. The katipo is the most poisonous spider in New Zealand — only the female can bite humans and it can be fatal, though hospitals carry an antidote. The spider is an endangered species.

Scrub

In New Zealand and Australia, low-growing vegetation regarded as being of no particular value is referred to as scrub. It consists of smaller plants, as opposed to the larger trees of the forest or bush. Scrub was often so dense it was impenetrable, and its removal to provide open farmland provided much work for scrub cutters.

Tuatara

Several of New Zealand's native creatures, such as kiwi, takahe and weta, are unusual, but the tuatara is probably the strangest of them all. It is a reptile, not a lizard, and is frequently referred to as a living fossil because it is closely related to other reptiles that died out a hundred million years ago. The mostly nocturnal tuatara grows very slowly and has an average age of 60 years, although some can live to be over 100.

One of New Zealand's most remarkable creatures, the slow-growing tuatara is a living link with the age of dinosaurs.

The shaky ISLES

Black sand

When Captain Cook was at Mercury Bay, Coromandel, in November 1769, he observed 'thrown upon the Shore in several places . . . quantities of Iron sand which is brought down out of the Country by almost every little frish water brook.'

Black sand is a feature of many of New Zealand's west coast beaches — containing iron oxide, it is also known as iron sand. It is formed by the grinding action of the sea eroding volcanic cliffs. Because of its dark colour the sand absorbs heat from the sun and can be uncomfortable to walk on — on hot days a pair of jandals may be essential.

Pounamu

On 31 January 1770 at Queen Charlotte Sound, Captain Cook (see page 286) learned the Maori name for the South Island, which he recorded as Tovy-poenammu. The name refers to the extremely hard stone pounamu — also known as greenstone — that is prized by Maori for tools and ornaments. The main source of pounamu for Maori was traditionally in North Westland.

Today, as in the past, pounamu is considered precious by Maori. It is considered a great honour to be given a polished pounamu carving to be worn around the neck. There is a widely held belief that a person must never buy greenstone for themselves — it should always be a gift — or it will bring bad luck.

Black sand on the Taranaki coastline, a section of the 750 kilometre strip of this iron-rich deposit which extends from Patea to North Cape.

The shaky ISLES

Mud pools

Mud pools are a distinctive feature of the thermal region around Rotorua. These result from steam deep in the earth, rising to the surface beneath pools of rainwater. Acidic gases attack rocks and produce clay, which mixes with the water to form the mud pool. Rising steam continues to heat the mud, causing the boiling and bubbling effects.

Many tourists flock to Rotorua every year to witness the fascinating sight of the bubbling mud. It's even possible to take some of the (cooled) mud home— it's believed to be great for the skin.

Geothermal activity

New Zealand's geothermal activity — located from south of Lake Taupo to White Island — played a major part in Maori traditions. It also made daily life easier, especially bathing and cooking. By the end of the nineteenth century the region of most activity had become a major tourist attraction and the thermal waters which were said to have healing properties attracted large numbers of people.

In the 1950s the potential for the underground activity to produce electricity was investigated. New Zealand's first and the world's second geothermal power station began operating at Wairakei in 1959 — the first had been built in Italy in 1911.

Earthquakes

New Zealand experiences upwards of 200 earthquakes each year, and the strongest since European settlement is believed to have been

New Zealand

The Pohutu Geyser, one of the attractions of the Whakarewarewa thermal reserve near Rotorua, in action in 1982.

The shaky ISLES 277

centred on Cook Strait, Wellington and southwest Wairarapa in 1855. That quake may have been responsible for one of New Zealand's less fortunate nicknames — the Shaky Isles. The worst tremor in terms of loss of life was the Napier earthquake of 3 February 1931 in which 256 people were killed. It is possible to 're-live' the Napier earthquake in the form of an interactive installation at Museum of New Zealand Te Papa Tongarewa.

Natural gas
....

New Zealand homes first began using gas for cooking and heating in the 1860s. At that stage the gas was produced from coal, at gasworks. In 1959 a field of natural gas was discovered at Kapuni in South Taranaki, followed in 1969 by the discovery of the offshore Maui field. With the construction of high-pressure transmission pipelines, by 1971 this natural gas was being supplied to Auckland, Wellington and other North Island centres for use in homes and industry. Much of this gas is now used for the generation of electricity.

Wind
....

Wind is a major part of New Zealand's weather. In fact, this country is a windy place because of its location in the roaring forties — a region in the Southern Hemisphere lying between latitude 40 and 50 degrees south — famous for its strong and prevailing westerlies.

It could be said that New Zealand experiences a range of climates because it is a long thin country with plenty of latitude. New Zealand's wind and weather come from all directions, but the most common wind is a westerly. Westerlies bring wet weather to the west side of the country and, subsequently, dry warm weather along the east coast. New Zealand can also expect northerlies that bring tropical air laden with water vapour, causing much of the country's flooding. Southerlies bring cold Antarctic air.

New Zealand's capital city has earned the nickname 'Windy Wellington' due to its precarious position at the edge of Cook Strait. There it is at the mercy of winds which are funnelled off the mountains that run the length of the North and South islands.

Canterbury Nor'wester

The most distinctive feature of Canterbury's climate is the nor-wester — it's a hot, dry wind that can blow for several days at a time. The winds begin to the west, out in the Tasman Sea, crossing the Southern Alps and then descending to the Canterbury Plains. Strong nor'westers can be very wearying, and they are followed by a cold sou'westerly.

Cyclone Bola

In March 1988 Cyclone Bola struck Hawke's Bay and Gisborne/East Cape, and the region experienced three days of non-stop torrential rain. States of emergency were declared, and the rain resulted in landslides, road closures and widespread flooding of farms and horticultural land. Winds of up to 100 kph were recorded, and the force of the cyclone was also felt as far north as Dargaville, in Northland, where the line carrying the main water supply was washed away with a bridge. Bola was one of the most damaging cyclones to hit New Zealand, and resulted in three deaths.

Southern Cross

First observed by European navigators in the late fifteenth century, the Southern Cross is a small constellation which is only able to be seen from the southern hemisphere. While sailing from England to New Zealand in late 1859, Samuel Butler wasn't impressed by it: 'The southern cross is a very great delusion. It isn't a cross. It is a kite, a kite upside down, an irregular kite upside down, with only three respectable stars and one very poor and very much out of place'.

Bombay Hills

About 50 kilometres south of Auckland is a range of hills known as the Bombay Hills or, simply, the Bombays. Named after the ship which brought settlers to the district in 1863, the hills form a physical boundary between Auckland and the Waikato. They also provide a sense of where Auckland ends and the rest of New Zealand begins. Thus Aucklanders might refer to all other New Zealanders — except Northlanders — as living south of the Bombays. Some say the more narrow-minded of them think that New Zealand stops at the hills. The opposite is also true and some people living south of the Bombay Hills are suspicious of anything, or anyone, originating from north of the Bombays.

East Cape

East Cape, north of Gisborne in the North Island, is the easternmost extremity of New Zealand. The cape was named by Captain James Cook (see page 287) on 30 October 1769.

Volcanic Plateau

The Volcanic Plateau is the area in the central North Island formed by the Taupo eruption, about 1800 years ago. It is distinguished by its geothermal activity, with hot steam and mud pools, and includes Lakes Taupo and Rotorua and other smaller lakes near Rotorua, the volcanic peaks of Tongariro, Ngauruhoe and Ruapehu, and the Raurimu Spiral on the main trunk line.

Cook Strait

New Zealand writer and wit Denis Glover described this country as 'two Islands separated only by the Union Steamship Company'. For some 70 years that company's ferries provided a vital link between the North and South islands, across Cook Strait. That stretch of water, about 20 kilometres wide at its narrowest point, has the reputation of being one of the roughest in the world, with fierce winds and strong currents.

Dutchman Abel Tasman sailed near Cook Strait in 1642, and in early 1770 Captain James Cook journeyed through the passage between the two islands. The strait was then named after Cook, probably by his fellow explorers. In 1866 a telegraphic cable crossed Cook Strait, and in 1965 a cable carried electricity between the two islands.

Southern Alps

The Southern Alps — usually known simply as the Alps — are an almost continuous mountain chain that runs from the southwest to the northeast of the South Island. The name usually refers to the central section of this Main Divide, which contains its highest peak,

Mount Cook. The Southern Alps were sighted by Abel Tasman in 1642, but were named by Captain James Cook (see page 286) in March 1770 while sailing up the west coast of the South Island.

Aoraki Mount Cook

Captain James Cook (see page 286) never sighted the mountain that was named in his honour in 1851. A massive avalanche in 1991 reduced the height of Australasia's highest peak by 10 metres and Mount Cook now stands at 3754 metres. In 1998 the mountain was renamed Aoraki Mount Cook, the original Maori name — Aoraki — means cloud piercer in the Ngai Tahu dialect.

The magnificent Southern Alps, named by Captain Cook, with Aoraki Mount Cook in the middle.

West Coast

The West Coast usually refers to the west side of the South Island. The name was first used by whalers, sealers and traders who began visiting the region in the early 1800s. The region's rich history of goldmining and other such industries, as well as its rugged landscape and isolation — it's across the Southern Alps from Canterbury — have caused the area to develop a strong local identity.

Gully

New Zealand's many steep-sided valleys and small ravines are generally known as gullies. In May 1790 Captain James Cook (see page 286) and Joseph Banks both recorded seeing 'gullies' in Australia, and by the 1830s the term was in use on this side of the Tasman, too.

High Country

In the South Island the High Country is the mountain foothills, as used for sheep farming. More specifically, it refers to the strip of land high on the eastern side of the Southern Alps, from Marlborough to Southland.

Hell-hole of the Pacific

From the early 1800s Kororareka in the Bay of Islands — now known as Russell — was a favourite port for whaling ships. It also attracted runaway sailors and escaped convicts from the penal colonies in Australia. Prior to British sovereignty in 1840 the settlement was known for its lawless behaviour and, so, earned its nickname — Hell-hole of the Pacific.

Down under

From the late nineteenth century 'down under' was a popular term for New Zealand and Australia, which are on the opposite side — underside — of the world from Britain.

The Antipodes

The term 'antipodean' is used to describe places diametrically opposite each other and so 'the Antipodes' it is applied to New Zealand and Australia, which are on the opposite side of the world from Britain.

Mainland

The South Island is larger than the North Island, which may explain why the former can be referred to as the mainland. Similarly, South Islanders can be known as mainlanders. The idea is maintained by the well-known Mainland range of cheeses.

Interisland

In the last quarter of the nineteenth century the term 'interisland' was used in reference to the islands of the greater Pacific. But by the early 1900s it was being applied to events held between the North Island and South Island of New Zealand, particularly sporting events, such as rugby, cricket and hockey matches.

By the 1960s the transport service across Cook Strait was known as the interisland ferry. This led to the use from 1989 of the name Interislander for the ferry service between the North and South islands.

The shaky ISLES 285

Gentle Annie

There are several places known as Gentle Annie in New Zealand. Some have been named ironically and are far from gentle on the traveller, such as sections of the winding roads in inland Hawke's Bay and west of Gisborne. The name probably comes from a popular song in the 1860s, brought to New Zealand by goldminers from California.

Central

The northwestern part of the Otago region is known simply as Central. While other parts of New Zealand are known as Central Canterbury, Central Hawke's Bay and Central Marlborough, for example, if someone is talking about Central they must mean Central Otago.

West Coaster

A person who is born or living on the West Coast is known as a West Coaster. Such persons are, like their region, said to be independent, resourceful and extremely friendly. The expression was in use by 1866 when a letter on the subject of safety at sea, published in a Nelson newspaper, was signed by 'An Old West Coaster'.

Captain James Cook

James Cook was the greatest European explorer of the Pacific, and the second European to discover New Zealand. He visited this country during the course of his three expeditions: on the *Endeavour* (1768–71), with the *Resolution* and *Adventure* (1772–75), and with the *Resolution* and *Discovery* (1776–79). Cook circumnavigated the North and South islands and produced a remarkably accurate chart of the coast. In this country he is remembered by a number of geographic features, including Cook Strait (see page 281), Cooks Cove, on the southern side of Tolaga Bay; Cooks Beach, on the Coromandel Peninsula; and two elevated points known as Mount Cook — the one in the Southern Alps (see page 281) and the other in Wellington City.

Image Credits

Alexander Turnbull Library: 9, 21, 27 Dominion Post Collection, 85 The Weekly News Collection, 89 John Selkirk/Dominion Post Collection, 95 Ross Giblin/Dominion Post Collection, 113 courtesy of Roger Donaldson, and the New Zealand Film Commission, 147 Tourism New Zealand, 174 Dominion Post Collection, 176, 183 Dominion Post Collection, 187 John Nicholson/Dominion Post Collection, 192, 201 Evening Post Collection, 224 New Zealand Free Lance Collection, 235, 241 New Zealand Free Lance Collection, 277 Department of Tourism, 285; **APN**: 151 Alan Gibson/*New Zealand Herald*; **Archives New Zealand**: 141; **Bell Tea Company Ltd**: 53; **Cadbury**: 45; **Foodstuffs Ltd**: 237; **Goodman Fielder**: 33; **Sam Harvey**: 39; **iStock**: 275, 280; **KiwiRail Ltd**: 254; **Learning Media Ltd**: 83 © Ministry of Education and published by Learning Media Ltd 1965; **Lion Nathan**: 24; **Lotteries Commission**: 129; **Ministry for Culture and Heritage**: 163; **Museum of New Zealand Te Papa Tongarewa**: 117 Gordon Burt; **Natural Sciences Image Library**: 207 GR 'Dick' Roberts/© Natural Sciences Image Library, 272 John Marris © Natural Sciences Image Library; **New Zealand Post**: 49, 210, 221; **Jim Pickles**: 103; **Rawleigh's Healthcare**: 23; **Reserve Bank of New Zealand**: 181; **Jeff Thomson**: 197; **Unilever**: 15; **Wattie's**: 240.